Schools: The Happiest Days of

Straight talk about finding optimism, resilience and flow in austerity Britain.

Veteris vestigia flammae

This book is dedicated in loving memory of Emma Frances Lee (1927- 2011) who always put the well-being of others before her own.

Acknowledgements

With thanks to Prof. Marty Seligman, Dr. Tal Ben Shahar, Prof. Felicia Huppert, Prof. Mark Williams, Dr. Colleen McLaughlin, Sir Ken Robinson, Dr Anthony Seldon, Dr. Oliver Bangham and Ian Morris, for their inspiration and contribution to the continuing debate about well-being in schools.

Thanks to pupils at Wellington College, Berkshire, UK and at Northwood Prep., Hertfordshire, UK. and special thanks to James Nutt for his art work - 'Self Portrait'.

Thanks to Nicole Pollock at Northwood for her editorial expertise and advice.

Special thanks to Ian and Heather at the GS Foundation for their kindness, support and generous sponsorship that has helped to spread the word.

CONTENTS

PREFACE   **PAGE**
THE REAL EASTENDERS
Learning resilience in the face of adversity 04

CHAPTER 1
Can happiness be taught? 11

CHAPTER 2
The central challenge of our times:
Defining a worthwhile life 17

CHAPTER 3
The rationale for pupil well-being lessons:
Defining well-being and happiness 30

CHAPTER 4
Background to the positive psychological approach 38

CHAPTER 5
Ten practical suggestions for school settings 51

CHAPTER 6
Positive Psychology – A stumbling block or stepping stone? 68

CHAPTER 7
Evaluating one school based well-being curriculum 75

CHAPTER 8
Conclusions 92

BIBLIOGRAPHY 100

Preface
The real Eastenders: learning resilience in the face of adversity.

Teaching is the prince of all professions, particularly appealing for those of us who began our teaching careers in the comprehensive schools of the late seventies, driven by a commitment to the possibility of creating a more equitable and happier world.

Over thirty years on, we now have the benefit of hindsight to evaluate the extent to which those dreams, channelled through the machinations and social experimentation of a succession of governments, have been realised.

*In that time we have seen almost three generations of children pass through the care of the schools where I have worked: the oldest children that I taught in 1979 are now fifty years old with grandchildren of their own. This book is a sincere attempt to capture some of the wisdom that this experience has afforded over time, in the hope that we can act on the accumulation of knowledge rather than passively allow history to repeat itself because
no-one listens.*

It is very difficult to overestimate the impact of our environment on our intellectual growth and development. For me, the experience of growing up as an authentic Eastender is vastly different from the curious depiction currently made popular on daily tv. My parents spent the vast majority of their lives in the Borough of Newham, being born there, marrying in 1950 and ultimately both passing away (with a gap of 32 years between my father in 1979 and then my mother in 2011) in the same house that they had occupied since the sixties.

I first made my way amongst blitz-damaged landscapes to school, as a five year old pupil, in September 1962 and, quite literally, have been going to school quite willingly, in some capacity or another, every day of my working life since. I was born with an atmosphere of war still in the air. Today we can become somewhat desensitised to the regular combat images from Iraq and Afghanistan, but some of us remember vividly the impact of the devastating effects of high explosives that fell on our own turf. People brought up in the East End had to be pretty tough. This bred a resilience of its own. To demonstrate that this is not an exaggeration, I was brought up in an area savagely bombarded in the Blitz. Our community was hit hard – just a mile down the road where I went to school arguably one of the most horrific and defining events of the entire Blitz took place. As a reporter in the Daily Herald of the day described, it was to another school in Agate Street, Canning Town, that 600 people had been led during the bombings on a Saturday night: families in an acute state of shock. Most had lost their homes; for some, members of their family had been killed or wounded, or were missing; they had few if any possessions; their clothes were torn and dirty, their faces blackened by smoke and soot, often caked with blood, their feet burned and lacerated. Terrified, confused, some hysterical, others racked with uncontrollable anger, others traumatized and unable to speak, they clung desperately to each other. These unfortunate people had been told to be ready for the coaches at three o'clock. Hours later the coaches had not arrived. Women were protesting with violence and with tears about the delay. The displaced East Enders were still huddled in the school at 8pm on Monday when the alert sounded. At 3.45 on the morning of Tuesday, September 10, a bomb scored a direct hit on South Hallsville School. Half the building was demolished, and hundreds of tons of masonry crashed down on its occupants.

It has never been established why the coaches did not arrive, but whatever the reason, the result was fatal – allegedly 450 dead. West Ham Council announced the death toll as 73, but to this day locals believe that hundreds perished in the school that night.

The tragedy of South Hallsville School

In the light of such a tragic experience of life and death, our current financial austerity in London is given some perspective. The fundamental truths remain the same. The lessons of how we have to pick ourselves up in times of greatest loss, when the circumstance of life drags us down deep, remain as fundamental now as then.

Thus my own experience of school could not be described as a privileged education: quite the reverse. For Newham was, and still is, one of the neediest boroughs in Greater London. Over 80% of the housing stock had been destroyed in many areas and it took decades for any meaningful improvements to be made in the social fabric. There is a huge debate about the place of the environment on the learning opportunities for our children – characterised by the discussion about the relative importance of nature or nurture – but the conditions experienced in post war docklands were arguably not the best antecedents for scholastic endeavour. It does not help when the educational policy makers muddy the waters by presiding over huge errors in process and direction. Taking the wreckage of South Hallsville School as a powerful metaphor for an education system that was once the pride of all systems worldwide, we still await a phoenix to arise from those ashes, where quality of education is assured despite the post-code, educational lottery that is being currently played out on a daily basis across the country.

What we in the local community in the East End did learn at that time was to organise ourselves to make the best of circumstances. To cut the long story of an educational experience short, I managed to get together enough educational qualifications to meet the criteria for teacher training, despite being caught up fair and square in a catastrophic re-organisation of the education system. This 'comprehensivisation' dismantled years of progression and advancement at a stroke, effectively removing the ladder of social mobility for future generations of bright, working class children in the immediate vicinity by destroying the high quality of teaching and learning previously on offer. The statistics of the failing schools tells a story of its own: compare the numbers of children achieving 5 pass General Certificate of Secondary Education grades at my old school in 1975 and its counterpart, still housed in the same buildings, in 2011 and you will see the extent of the decline.

Many grammar schools in the area were dismantled, with a severe blow to any concept of meritocracy as I could see it, and in schools that symbolised a severely mis-shapen, malformed, utopian vision of 'equality', quickly levelled down all semblance of academic standards and civilised behaviour: schools in my home town became battlegrounds, between teachers and pupils and pupils and their peers, particularly between the local white population (it was the time of the rise of the notorious skinhead culture) and the many ethnic minorities who had increasingly made East London their home. In the meantime, many of the good teachers in the system 'headed for the hills,' as did many aspirational white families. Crudely described as 'white flight' in many urban landscapes throughout the world, any hopes of a fully integrated society have been put on hold.

All was not lost. Much will be said about resilience later in this book, but avoiding empty triumphalism, this narrative is a personal example, for anyone interested in learning the facts about a sixties, urban education, of resilience, of the potential for personal development even in reduced circumstances.

It is said apocryphally that the battle of Waterloo might have been won on the playing fields of Eton, but organisation, fair play, synergy, courage, teamwork and other key lessons in life were also formulated and established on lesser grass patches, such as Brampton Park, The Terence Macmillan stadium and the fields of Flanders Rd., E6. For this unpromising beginning did not stifle in me an innate sense of creativity that was recognised and mentored by many in the teaching community.

Despite losing out initially in the postcode lottery, I had always been a performer from the earliest stages of my education. My county rugby performances led to a description in the Daily Telegraph of my contribution as a 'very mobile hooker' (sic). My athletic abilities were coached on many sports fields throughout the country - county, regional and national honours in rugby union beckoned.

This experience of life was supported in terms of aesthetics and culture: I performed in orchestras where I managed, despite a fair amount of peer group banter, to become a proficient violinist and vocalist, performing in London at the Royal Festival Hall. I felt equally at home on the stage, with early opportunities to perform the plays of Hans Christian Anderson, Shakespeare and the Capek Brothers that helped broaden my knowledge and understanding of the world. These comments are not included here as some form of self-aggrandisement but merely to depict accurately the benefits of an education that caters appropriately for all aspects of our personality and character – we might call this roundedness – even for those living in humble circumstances. All things are possible, given the encouragement of the appropriate values – commitment, curiosity, persistence.

All these rich and varied experiences were nurtured and encouraged by passionate and encouraging teachers. In turn, the teaching profession gave me the full opportunity to share these passions with the young. Teaching for me has always been a vocation, schools becoming a workplace where I have felt most at home, the arena that made the most authentic use of what I consider to my signature strengths. It has been an occupation and a pre-occupation for me, grabbing my attention both at school and at home, demanding of my full effort and enthusiasm during term times as well as school holidays, and impacting on my family life as well as my professional activities.

It also has made possible a hugely rewarding life-time journey of learning that has taken me to the exalted high table of a Cambridge education, the novelty of being addressed as Doctor following a lengthy period of educational research, despite having no medical training, the authorship of books and learned journals, the opportunity to lecture extensively in the UK, States and Canada, and the privilege of leading a school that has been recently described as outstanding in all aspects of its provision by the Inspectorate. Along the way, there have been enormously enjoyable social moments when I have dined with Olympic athletes, played team sport for charity alongside World Cup winners, shared drinks with the Queen's consort, spent a very pleasant hour as escort to the Queen's cousin, dined at the Inner Temple and at 10 Downing Street, entertained a Crown Prince and Princess from a European state, made friends with Peers of the realm: quite a journey.

After thirty two years, this passion for teaching and learning continues to burn brightly. The young energise and invigorate teachers, and you find the requisite emotional energy even when you begin to flag. There is no bigger thrill than to see a generation proceed through school from reception to Year Eight, first as innocent, demanding three year olds, all the way through to calm, confident and accomplished young men at thirteen. There is huge joy to be had in explaining a complicated concept to my pupils, addressing a problem from a number of angles until they achieve that 'light bulb' moment. There is equal pleasure in helping pupils resolve issues and emotional problems that they might be having at school, to be a cheer-leader, mentor, coach, authority figure and friend.

Furthermore, as I have developed in a life time career in teaching, opportunities for leadership have beckoned and this has brought with it the biggest challenges and joys in equal measure. I have thrived in working through the practicalities of leading two schools, getting them ready for the visits of inspectors, motivating teaching staff, encouraging an effective and efficient school administration, dealing with the cares and concerns of demanding parents, satisfying the demands of a discerning governing body as well as being responsible for the leadership of the learning in all its different facets of the pupils in my charge. These are not light responsibilities and after twenty five years of senior management there are more lines on the face as aspects of the role become more burdensome: but the honest truth is that not many of the class of '79 at teacher training college would have chosen a different vocational direction.

The world has clearly changed from the one we knew in 1979. As I began my teaching career, many would argue that information technology had not really been invented, there were no ipods because the Sony Walkman had just been launched. Those who grew up on a diet of westerns at the Saturday morning pictures mourned the loss of John Wayne. For those interested in music, it was the age of punk rock, Sid Vicious was found dead in New York and 'Y.M.C.A.' was the top selling hit of the year in the UK. Further afield, this was the year that Mother Teresa won the Nobel Peace Prize

Perhaps most significantly from an educational viewpoint, Margaret Thatcher became Britain's first female Prime Minister. We are still working through the sea-changes brought about by her administration. Early changes introduced were a new vocational training and the introduction of the Assisted Places Scheme.

Importantly, new initiatives were on the horizon that were to cause turbulence as never witnessed before. The 1988 Education Reform Act made considerable changes to the education system. These changes were aimed at creating a 'market' in education with schools competing with each other for 'customers' (pupils). A new form of natural selection came into being, reflecting the theory that bad schools would lose pupils to good schools and would either have to improve, reduce in capacity or close in the process .The reforms included the introduction of a National Curriculum that made it compulsory for schools to teach certain subjects and syllabuses. Previously, the choice of subjects had been up to the school. National curriculum assessments were introduced at the Key Stages 1 to 4 (ages 7, 11, 14 and 16 respectively) through what were formerly called Standard Assessment Tests (SATS). At Key Stage 4 (age 16), the assessments were made from the GCSE exam.

Formula funding was introduced, which meant that the more children a school could attract to it, the more money it got. Open Enrolment and choice for parents were brought back, so that parents could choose or influence which school their children went to.

League tables began showing performance statistics for each school, another theme that will be commented on here. These are regularly published in a selection of newspapers and on the internet, so parents and the public can see results for schools in each area of the country. What many cannot see is how fatuous league table comparisons have become, particularly in the ridiculous way they reduce a child's school experience to a grade in an examination at a key stage - as if every school is operating on a level playing field. It does not. Schools are led differently, are organised in more or less efficient ways and attract students with a variety of social backgrounds and educational needs.

Schools could, if enough of their pupils' parents agreed, opt out of local government control, becoming grant maintained schools and receiving funding directly from central government. The government offered more money than the school would get usually from the local authority as an enticement. This was seen as a political move given that often local authorities were not run by the governing Conservative Party whereas central government was.

These were weighty changes. We all have a tendency to look at the past through rose tinted lenses, as if the past was a golden age. We overlook the very real difficulties and challenges. If anything, professional life in the world of education in 1979 was less complicated. We were less reflective in an age of increasing prescription. Regulatory requirements had not gotten out of hand, although the authority of the teacher was quickly ebbing away in the comprehensive school where I began my career.

At the start of my professional life I went to work in a town where a successful voluntary aided school had previously stood, and a new, all-boys' comprehensive soon foundered. It was a social experiment that did not work, for the simple reason that it did not capture the sensitivities, hearts and minds of the pupils involved, who quickly realised that, in terms of authority and discipline, the king wore no clothes. The out playing of this general erosion of corporate discipline accompanied by the distain for authority was a distant foreshadowing yet potent foretaste of the horrifying rioting on the streets of London, Birmingham and the North in August, 2011. There was seemingly nothing that an enfeebled leadership team that was high on rhetoric but less effective on process or practice could do to create the necessary order or discipline. The initial rules of engagement were drawn up: an initial battle of the wills was fought over the right of a boy to wear an ear-ring to school. When this initial skirmish was lost, six weeks into the creation of the new establishment, the writing was literally on the wall: vandalism was rampant and the pupils had very little pride in their school and less respect for their teachers. The new facilities quickly became shabby, broken down and covered in graffiti.

The morale of teachers was eroded and there was a rush to read the Times Educational Supplement on a Friday to find a route, any route, out of the situation. Some teachers left to sell dubious financial products that very soon crashed below their purchase price, alienating them to the family members and friends who had been gullible enough to invest without due diligence.

I was part of an unofficial escape committee. We knew things could be run better than this. An era of strikes was ushered in. Quickly the school fell into disrepair and a once highly prized status in the locality was reduced to disrepute. Interestingly, under new organisation, structures and a new leadership, the school later has become a flagship. Sacrificing a generation of pupils was far too high a price to pay and those responsible for this ill-conceived, failed social experiment should hang their heads in shame.

Over thirty years have elapsed and with the passage of time and significant social change, it is urgently necessary to review again what the key purposes of an education in contemporary, austerity Britain should look like. This book attempts to describe one particularly fertile area of discussion that should be a concern for all those involved in improving schools and family life in our current era, namely the well-being of the children involved. There has undoubtedly been a spiralling down in many of our schools and the statistics are shocking.

On January 9th 1979, the Music for UNICEF Concert was held at the United Nations General Assembly to raise money for UNICEF and promote the Year of the Child. Forwarding the clock nearly 30 years, it was not fund-raising that caught my attention. UNICEF were to have a profound effect on my thinking for entirely different reasons. In many ways the social world for children of school age has changed and UNICEF were to highlight some significant features of contemporary life that both shock and disturb in equal measure. This has caused some of us to re-evaluate our mission, vision and values, with surprising and unpredictable results.

The author with children in the Kayamandi township, South Africa, January 2012

Chapter 1: Can happiness be taught?

As school teachers, we are not often afforded the luxury of time to consider the bigger picture about what we are all trying to achieve – we have classes to teach, budgets to organise, parents, staff and pupils to meet. We can all sympathise about time pressure in austerity Britain – there is always more to do at work than time allows. In the last five years, however, I have been fortunate enough, through my travels as part of my educational research, to have shared rich conversations with other colleagues involved in education, from all over the world. I have visited educational settings as far afield as Harrow on the Hill to the Kayamandi Township in Stellenbosch, South Africa, and from the quiet and reflective medieval courts of Jesus College, Cambridge to the raw realities of schools in Boston Mass. where families are often at direct risk of gun crime.

What amazes me is the way in which beliefs about the central purpose of our work in schools are still heavily contested. Could it be that our fundamental beliefs about the purpose and function of education have been blurred in the race for league table positions based on exam results? This places teachers who hold a broader view of the purpose of education in a dilemma: the purpose they give to education is often at variance to the meaning assigned by other members of society. For example, after many years of central government obsession with testing, there is a strong desire in many for more freedom.

In response, this book is a call to action for teachers and school leaders to find time in their busy schedules to review their own priorities and to reflect on why we were called to do this work in the first place. Notwithstanding the hollow rhetoric about the development of all aspects of the educational experience provided for pupils contained in many school promotional web-sites, prospectuses and mission statements, it can be argued that it is the statistically measurable content of assessments that is one of the principle drivers of education currently in the UK. As Peters reminds us (1986), '**What gets measured, gets done**'. Our materialistic society may also subscribe to an even more damming, positivistic epithet that suggests that whatever cannot be measured does not even exist. I suggest that sometimes we have to use a telescope to see the bigger educational landscape rather than be always enslaved by the use of the microscope of data analysis in our path to school improvement.

We in the UK have suffered from initiative overload for decades – the list is endless as well as mostly fruitless - but there is a stirring in government that chimes with the current spirit of the age in a time of economic austerity. As a result, the Office for National Statistics are leading a debate called the National Well-being Project which will seek to establish the key areas that matter most to people's well-being. The pursuit for a better understanding of what makes for a fuller and more satisfying life has a profound impact on teachers as we substitute the vague notion of 'happiness' with the compound noun 'well-being'. This leads us to consider a vital question that all of us involved in schools and families need to answer regarding the nature and dimensions of happiness and pupil well-being.

Can happiness be taught? Possibly not, just in the same way as it cannot be marketed in bottle size units or produced under laboratory conditions. This does not remove the moral duty for us to do everything we can to make our schools happy places in which to work and study, where there is a sense of psychological safety, where children and staff can interact positively and constructively to become the best learners and teachers possible. This aim is achievable despite the context in which the school finds itself. It is not the province purely for the wealthy middle class establishments, or the independent sector, for colleagues such as Sir Michael Wilshaw, the Chief Inspector of Schools, has shown that an orderly, productive and positive educational environment can be created even in the neediest and impoverished social circumstances.

There is general agreement that childhood should be a time of curiosity, a time of innocence, fun and laughter. Childhood is a formative period when our characters and personalities are moulded and shaped, hopefully in supportive and loving conditions where children are welcomed and accepted. School days can be the happiest days of our lives when we are untrammeled by the need to make money, where every day can be an adventure, where there are new things to learn and new friendships to establish. In this rather idealized vision, schools can play an essential role by being places of nurture and growth, where personal knowledge, skill and understanding are advanced by kindly yet authoritative, caring and effective teachers.

We all know of people, and we may well be included in the list, for whom school was an entirely unhappy affair because of a host of contributory factors: uncaring teachers pouring out derision, the prevalence of a pernicious bullying culture, weak leadership or a meaningless curriculum. Many still live under the shadow of unhelpful things said at school either by teachers or fellow pupils and there are some resonances here for many of us. The better news is that, informed by thirty years of daily experience in schools, I can say with confidence that it does not have to be like this.

Schools are, obviously, incredibly social places where happy and positive people can have a tremendous impact on young people as they offer direction about the right paths to travel. Lively, personable, kindhearted, altruistic and caring people have infectious personalities. They can make a real impact on any organization: the 'happiness bug' can be caught if the overarching ethos of a school, set by the school leadership, creates the necessary conditions for infectious happiness and appreciation to spread. If it is at all possible, it seems to me that it is feasible and desirable in our teaching to recognize the scientifically credible constituents of happiness that can be shared in classes as we aim to be true to our vocation and make an authentic, positive difference to the life experiences of our pupils.

Some sad truths

The August riots of 2011 created a shock wave across the nation and indeed around the world. Since then there has been much soul-searching as well as some fairly feeble quasi-sociological reasons offered to explain some of the worst examples of social unrest, arson, looting and, ultimately, murder on the streets of some major English cities. This anti-social behaviour adds a sense of urgency to the debate.

I think it is vital to actively promote pupil well-being for a number of reasons, despite the complexities involved. At the core of this argument is the notion that developing a holistic approach, where due regard is given to pupil well-being, should become a key aim. As a matter of urgency, we need to embed proven courses such as the Penn State Resilience Programme and the Wellington College Well-Being Course into the mainstream curriculum, after giving our teachers sufficient training to deliver it. This must happen now: we cannot afford to wait any longer. The dilemma is that teachers have been pushed from pillar to post in order to deliver one spurious measure of performance at all costs, namely key stage assessments and GCSE passes at A* -C, fuelled by the mindless league table mentality that proliferates in austerity Britain. If we had thought more creatively about the proper purposes of schooling, we may well be in a different place.

We do not have to go far to find some very persuasive statistical data to demonstrate just how far we have fallen back in promoting and nurturing the well-being of our children in contrast to other wealthy nations. As a result, we cannot duck the issue any longer.

In February 2007, a UNICEF report on 'child well-being in rich countries' placed the UK as the worst out of 21 countries. Children in the UK were found to engage in very high levels of risky behaviour in the unholy quartet of drinking, drugs, smoking and sex. The UK was found to have high levels of children with no parent in employment; high numbers of stepfamilies and single-parent families; and high numbers of households with fewer than 10 books. A more detailed description is provided below:

Dimension 4 - Family & peer relationships
Top: Italy — *Bottom*: United Kingdom
Family structure
- % of children living in single-parent families.
- % of children living in stepfamilies.

Family relationships
- % of children who report eating the main meal of the day with parents more than once a week.
- % of children who report that parents spend time 'just talking' to them.

Peer relationships
- % of 11, 13 and 15 year-olds who report finding their peers 'kind and helpful'.

Dimension 5 - Behaviours and risks
Top: Sweden — *Bottom*: United Kingdom
Health behaviours
- % of children who eat breakfast.
- % who eat fruit daily.
- % physically active.
- % overweight.

Risk behaviours
- % of 15 year-olds who smoke.
- % who have been drunk more than twice.
- % who use cannabis.
- % having sex by age 15.
- % who use condoms.
- teenage fertility rate.

Experience of violence
- % of 11, 13 and 15 year olds involved in fighting in last 12 months.
- % reporting being bullied in last 2 months.

Dimension 6 - Subjective well-being
Top: Netherlands — *Bottom*: United Kingdom
Health
- % of young people rating their own health no more than 'fair' or 'poor'.

School life
- % of young people 'liking school a lot'.

Personal well-being
- % of children rating themselves above the mid-point of a 'Life Satisfaction Scale'.
- % of children reporting negatively about personal well-being.

Critics of the report might say that the statistics are flawed or incomplete, the methodologies used to collect the data are not compelling, and the sample is not representative. The straightforward response is that there is no smoke without fire whatever our critical proclivities or own personal biases. The telling statistic is that when children were asked to make judgments of their health, school life and satisfaction, the UK came at the bottom of the pile for any sense of well-being. We simply cannot ignore these shocking findings.

To a great extent this report has been largely ignored. Collectively, we cannot believe it and it is far easier for us to bury our head in the sand than admit the difficulty that we are in. Four years on from the UNICEF report, the headlines have come and gone. We shake our heads in self-denial, momentarily hold our heads in a moment of pseudo-guilt before looking up and continuing with business as usual. What will it take before we act? Do we have to wait for the disease to become end-stage before we make any real effort to address the causes of the malaise? It is time to apply our creativity in new and meaningful ways to address causes and not just symptoms.

My own experience is that I began a professional teaching career in 1979 with a specific vocational commitment to contribute to pupils' broader educational experience – as inspectors of schools we call this social, moral, spiritual and cultural education. This involved the delivery of a variation of the curriculum that Professor Andy Hargreaves at Toronto calls the Julie Andrews model: 'here are a few of my favorite things'. This was curricular design by necessity: in order to capture the attention of a diffident and sometimes outright aggressive pupil cohort, topics were introduced that covered controversial or catastrophic behaviours, that held some kind of base appeal. It is well-accepted that such shock tactics in health education very rarely succeed in achieving their objective (see Lee, 1992). People believe that the consequences of risky behaviour will never happen to them.

This model was profoundly flawed, for it introduced the pupils to a catastrophic list of worst case scenarios that pupils had to avoid at all cost if they were to live fulfilling and happy lives. This well-meaning but misguided principle may well still be reflected in the methodology and syllabi of social, moral, spiritual and citizenship education topics in schools throughout the UK: drug abuse, sexually transmitted diseases, arguments for and against abortion, arguments for and against smoking, the argument for euthanasia etc. This is not to say that there should not be a place in the curriculum for pupils to be aware of the riskier elements of human behaviour as well as possible consequences. The argument here is that there has to be a positive message that can be put across in a more effective way by appealing to the better aspects of the human condition. The learning objective has to be constructive.

For those of us charged with the responsibility of educating the young, ignoring the warning signs could easily be construed as one of the biggest crimes of the century. Because we choose, at our own extreme peril, to fail to acknowledge the writing on the wall, we are effectively continuing to create the conditions for social and economic disaster.

As we struggle with the difficulties of the current economic downturn, and rioting on the streets, we need no other wake-up call: we are cultivating a generation of young people who are unhealthily unhappy, who engage in risky behaviour for a host of reasons, who have poor relationships with their family and their peers, who have low expectations of school and life who don't feel safe.

Despite the huge sums spent on state education by the tax-payer, the end product is of a hugely varied quality, dependent often on where you live and what the quality of the leadership is like in the local school. Many would argue that we are not getting value for money. There is little evidence of leading, creative thinking or intelligent debate being applied to the problems that are besetting the educational establishment in the country. We do not have a fully joined up, coherent system for the seventeen years that constitute a child's experience from nursery to graduation. There are still too many variables. What was once the envy of the world is now being over taken, particularly by countries to the East who recognise the prime importance of softer, interpersonal skills as opposed to our fixation on examinations and assessments. We are rapidly in danger of losing the right to sit at the world's scholastic top table.

It is time for corporate action to begin to address the issues, without the usual discourse of blame. This is too important a subject to be ignored. It cuts across government boundaries and is too vital to be kicked around as a party political football as an excuse to score points. It will take a concerted effort by all concerned – families, schools, governments, businesses, all those with leadership capacity, the church – but an obvious starting point would be to review our provision in schools and attempt to adopt a new approach.

We are cultivating a generation of young people who are unhealthily unhappy

Chapter 2: The central challenge of our times: defining a worthwhile life

Surely happiness is of central importance to all of us. Who does not want to be happy and wish the same for their loved ones? It would be wrong, of course, to suggest that the desire for happiness is located solely in the province of a twenty first century society, often rooted in hedonism, the logical conclusion to a 'me first' society. The pursuit of happiness, in itself, is not a new quest. Ever since we have considered, recorded and reflected in a systematic way, the question of what makes people happy has been of primary importance: even in the years before the birth of Christ, Aristotle talked about 'eudemonia' – happiness as human flourishing and purpose to life. To me this stands in stark contrast to the prevailing orthodoxy, the prevalent, modern hedonistic concept that the worthwhile life, the happiest existence, is where the one who collects the most toys, wins. For Aristotle, happiness was the meaning and purpose of life, the whole aim and end of human existence. His assumption was that although people value fame, health and riches because we hope they will make us happy, we should value happiness for itself, its own sake, as the only worthwhile intrinsic goal.

As we seek for further examples to support this happiness thesis, one of the conclusions of Enlightenment thinkers such as Hume and de Montesquieu was that the pursuit of happiness was the basis of social well-being and personal motivation (Csikszentmihalyi 1999). This is condensed by John Locke (1690) when he said that 'what we call good which is apt to cause or increase pleasure or diminish pain'. He also realized the need for the pursuit of happiness through prudence, a message lost on today's materialistic worldview.

Bentham (1789) insisted that a good society allows the greatest happiness for the greatest number. It is not surprising, therefore, to see these ideologies underpin an increase in affluence and control over the material world with the mistaken view that materialism is the high road to happiness. With this commonplace ideology, the dominating and domineering thoughtless hedonism of this age has trivialized the truth of the Aristotelian paradigm. Our culture has a restricted repertoire where so many people feel that their only hope for a happy life is to amass as much as they can, as quickly as they can.

Championing the pursuit of happiness became enshrined later as one of the responsibilities of a just and worthy government, encapsulated in the Declaration of Independence of the United States. This theme was revisited powerfully by Bobby Kennedy (1968)

> *'Too much and for too long, we seem to have surrendered personal excellence and community value in the mere accumulation of material things. Our Gross National Product... ...counts air pollution and cigarette advertising and ambulances to clear our highways of carnage. It counts special locks for our doors and the jails for the people who break them. It counts the destruction of the redwoods and the loss of our natural wonder in chaotic sprawl. It counts napalm and it counts nuclear warheads, and armored cars for the police to fight riots in our cities.*
>
> *Yet the Gross National Product does not allow for the health of our children, the quality of their education, or the joy of their play. It does not include the beauty of*

> *our poetry or the strength of our marriages, the intelligence of our public debate or the integrity of our public officials. It measures neither our wit nor our courage, neither our wisdom nor our learning, neither our compassion nor our devotion to our country; it measures everything, in short, except that which makes life worthwhile.'*

What makes life worthwhile? Kennedy had good ideas about the ingredients of a happy and worthy life: **the health of our children and the quality of their education and play** are integral to his vision for a happy society. What is it, then, forty plus years on from this dramatic speech, that continues to make life worthwhile? With the massive increase in knowledge afforded by the internet revolution, what have we really learned since the death of Kennedy?

Today, many have a tendency to effectively reduce everything to a common cash equivalent. Experience in school demonstrates that our children quickly evaluate the cost of everything but struggle to appreciate value. This is the thin end of the wedge as we begin to make broader value judgements based on this premise. The worth of a person quickly then becomes determined by the price achieved in modern marketplaces. High net worth individuals become the paradigm of success regardless of the quality of their interpersonal relationships or general happiness in life. Entry to the Sunday Times rich list becomes the highest aspiration possible. No-one can claim to be wise unless they can demonstrate that a high price can be charged for a consultation.

The sad fact is that we only have a finite amount of energy and enthusiasm and as we invest it in the pursuit of wealth, we have less time to pursue other worthier goals that are necessary for a happy existence. This is all happening against a backdrop where the evidence is that the relationship between wealth and happiness in tenuous at best (Csikszentmihalyi 1999). This book will suggest that the importance we attribute to money itself, rather than the amounts we possess, is the greatest influence on our happiness (see Seligman 2002).

A materialistic lifestyle seems to be counterproductive because **with the exception of those in the extremes of poverty**, people who seem to desire to accumulate money more than other life goals are least satisfied with their life experience. There seems to be abundant proof that the biblical maxim that the love of money is the root of all kinds of evil, holds water. We adapt to whatever our current levels of wealth provide all too quickly. If we are not vigilant, we habituate: life becomes a hedonic treadmill where the material wealth we accumulate raises our expectations and leaves us no better off in terms of our well-being than we were before. We become like hamsters on a wheel, going nowhere fast. Or we see acts of desperation, demonstrating the worst elements of groupthink, when hordes join the queues of other looters who falsely believe that stealing a 52 inch flat-screen from Comet in the August riots is somehow going to make them happier.

A spark of optimism

Yet, at the beginning of the second decade of the new millennium, there may be a small spark of optimism as the quest for the holy grail of personal happiness and fulfilment is being seriously revisited in different quarters. This can only come from a realization that much of what we desire is related to finding happiness in meaning and purpose, spirituality, creativity, compassion, wisdom, satisfying relationships, the ability to tolerate distress, feeling a sense of competence and achieving personal mastery.

Leaders in the modern world continue to grapple with issues of meaning, value and worth. For today, even the Prime Minister is trying to draw attention to this concept despite us all being in the midst of public service cuts and spiralling living costs. Speaking at the Google Zeitgeist Europe conference (2006), David Cameron commented:

> *'Well-being can't be measured by money or traded in markets. It's about the beauty of our surroundings, the quality of our culture and, above all, the strength of our relationships. Improving our society's sense of well-being is, I believe,* **the central political challenge of our times.***'*

The first findings from the Government's national well-being survey (Office for National Statistics) are beginning to emerge. One interesting fact is that London is the richest region in the UK but is not the happiest of populations. Respondents from the capital seem to have scored poorly on the key well-being indicators.

One of the most important tasks for educators, then, is to offer a better understanding of the dynamics of happiness. Teachers, who share a common vocation that exceeds the mere transmission of facts, should try to do their part to help prevent the disillusionment that comes from a fixation with the materialistic lifestyle. There is an escalation of expectations in austerity UK whereby we have a tendency to get habituated with current levels of affluence and we hanker for more. This seems to be a prime motivation amongst the wide spectrum of individuals who have taken to rioting on the streets and looting shops. Enough is never enough. We compare our possessions with those who have more and the phenomenon of relative deprivation seems too entrenched.

As our energy and interest is invested in generating more wealth, we have less time and enthusiasm for sensitivity to other interests including nature, art, literature and our religious faith. If we are not very careful, we can easily be addicted to material rewards where more becomes better and we become blind, losing the ability to become happy from other sources, such as time with our family and wider social groups.

The question above all questions then becomes,' how we can ourselves and other individuals, communities, and society become happier?'

A modern paradox: why children need to experience failure.

It can be argued that three modern forces have converged to cause an epidemic of depression, particularly in a previously prosperous UK. Simply put, it is the result of the

- greater emphasis on the individual,
- the erosion of shared social experiences and
- the priority on developing high self-esteem.

In the straining to achieve self-esteem in children too quickly, Seligman (2002) believes that there has been an emphasis on how the child feels at the expense of what the child does - mastery, persistence, overcoming frustration and boredom, and meeting challenge. This has left children without confirmation in the real world. The possible inconsistency between what the child is told and what is experienced about the self, can lead to confusion and mistrust. This societal priority emerged even though self-esteem is a product of success, not a cause. I would argue quite strongly that self-control and the ability to be persistent in tasks is surely a better predictor of success in life than self-esteem.

Seligman has important things to say to a modern generation of parents who seem to display little common sense in trying to shelter their children from every chill wind that blows, missing the point that these are in fact growth points. **Children need to fail.** If they get all that they want, all of the time, then this breeds a sense of entitlement. They need to feel sad, anxious and angry. Sheltering our children may eradicate wisdom and development as well as pain. If we leap in to bolster self-esteem to soften the blows when they encounter obstacles, we make it harder for them to achieve mastery.

None of these steps can be circumvented. If the expectation is that we should all have the best things in life laid on a plate, when we do not get them, this may well lead to the type of looting that we saw on the streets of Enfield, Tottenham, Wolverhampton and Manchester. Failure and feeling bad are necessary building blocks for ultimate success and feeling good. By encouraging success at low cost, we are in danger of creating a generation of very expensive failures.

If we are not careful, our children will graduate with a highly over-inflated sense of their worth to the world. I concur with the idea that pupils should not have their self-esteem artificially inflated without merit, or be raised to have a sense of entitlement.
We are already suffering from a politically correct culture where there are no designated losers any more. Everyone is a winner, no matter what the test, task, game, sport or competition. Everybody wins, everybody gets the certificate. No one is a loser but the last in the winners' list. No child these days will get to hear those all-important, crucial character-building words, 'You lost, Jonny!'

A lot of these pupils will never get to hear the truth about themselves until they are in their twenties. Of course, Jonny's parents can't understand why he is fired from his job for underachieving and why, after a failed marriage and a string of questionable affairs, he cannot form a meaningful, long lasting relationship. Or why he is appearing on a wanted poster for looting shops. In school he was always on the winners' rostrum because the parents ensured it was his entitlement. What they do not understand, of course, is that in many schools, everyone is on the winner's rostrum, if such outdated and politically incorrect edifices still exist, outside of Formula 1 racing and the Olympics.

My wife and I have brought up two children – now aged 28 and 26 at the time of writing - and I am no different from others in wanting to remove all adversity and difficulty in their life. Be that as it may, if I was to re-write their biographies, I would not remove their failures in the hope that I could teach them directly. Life's important lessons cannot be imparted as there is no direct correlation between telling our children one thing and they immediately learning that lesson for life. Knowledge, indeed wisdom, has an experiential element despite the fact that we would like to short-cut life's hardships for our kids. We have to be there to help interpret life's hardships with a sense of balance. Things do not always happen for the best, but we have to be those people who find the best in everything.

My mind wanders at this point to reflect on the times that I have felt a failure and felt it acutely. I was overlooked for a primary school award for achievement because I made some unguarded comments about another child's work. This cast a small shadow. One of the great things about a musical interest is that it introduced you to girls as well as Gershwin. My first romantic attachment with the leader of the orchestra was a disappointment and that too provided a steep emotional learning curve. The East End of London, despite the fictional depiction on East Enders on national television, was the ultimate reality show and could be a cruel training ground. What was perceived as a weakness, as different from the norm in terms of attitude or behaviour, was not tolerated particularly well. This was groupthink at its worse and not the most fertile ground for developing a sense of creativity.

One fundamental protective feature that shone through this period was the wealth of social capital, the rich resources that I accumulated by interacting with others, provided principally through a loving family where both parents were present and played a part in our up-bringing. This was supported by a strong church community at the local parish church where I was fully involved in the choir and scouts. Added to this was a rich vein of cultural capital, the information and resources that enrich our individual lives, where the grammar school unashamedly invited us to partake, through literature and the arts, in an introduction of enriching and enlightening intellectual and aesthetic activities. These support systems no doubt provided a degree of psychological capital, a sense of appreciation, a soft inoculation in the form of inner security, a good sense of attachment as well as the traits of resolve and resilience in the face of difficulty.

Money was in short supply, yet at no time did it enter our heads to steal: we took action in more productive ways. We improvised, even if it meant selling freshly cut sticks of rhubarb door to door and taking up a paper delivery round. We had enough and did not seem to crave a lot more. At no time did we feel that life owed us a living, neither did we feel victims of our environment. There was never a feeling of entitlement. Perhaps the advertising industry was underdeveloped: we certainly had no craving for high status fashion items.

We just got on with it. A good education was provided at primary level and in the preparation for ordinary level examinations, gave us the tools for self-realization and the possibilities for self-actualization. We can begin to see some of the fundamentals for the successful preparation for adult life even in these challenging circumstances.

I have never suffered from clinical depression but I do recognize that the times that I have felt most ill at ease with myself were times, often during the long vacation when I have felt most self-absorbed. I have tended to think about how I feel a great deal, and have detected sadness or ill health and ruminated on it. This has been an unhealthy self-absorption which is in complete contrast to the mental state I experience, described by the psychologists as flow, often when engaged in my hobby of fishing. When I am out on the reservoir there is a distinct lack of self-consciousness and more engagement. It is easy to find flow there, time stands still, is immaterial in the concentration in the task at hand. The hours fly by, a sense of self is lost. A sense of gratification does require some skill and effort and sometimes failure when the fish don't bite and when the weather turns unexpectedly nasty.

Pleasure seeking is a powerful motivating force in austerity Britain, but it does not produce lasting change in its search for comfort and relaxation. The gratifications can be stressful at times but can bring with them a sense of exhilaration rarely experienced at other times. Seligman shows that to ask the question about how I can be happy without distinguishing between pleasure and gratification is wrong because it leads to all kinds of short cuts. The greatest sense of well-being is to be found in the quest for a meaningful life, not the pleasurable one alone. At the other end of the spectrum, unwarranted self-esteem, self-absorbed individualism and a sense of being a victim has led to unprecedented levels of depression.

Research (Seligman 2002) suggests that unwarranted high self-regard can lead to violent and criminal behaviour. A straightforward approach says that instead of pushing for self-esteem, parents and educators should be teaching **optimism, resilience and self-control**.

A cry for help? Linking pessimism and depression.

Despite the recognition through this glimpse of the history of human sciences that happiness is fundamental and the pursuit of happiness is a central goal of life, it appears that there have been modest advancements in understanding the formula or necessary conditions that promote well-being and how we share these fundamental truths with the next generation. This surely must be a new emphasis for those teaching the young.

It seems to me that we are all on a happiness continuum, with all the vicissitudes, struggles and hardships that are part and parcel of all life, and a lifelong exploration of thinking, feeling and doing. The pursuit of happiness for all of us is exactly that – a pursuit. This book is not about five easy steps to self-help. It is the result of reflections during a lifetime in the education profession, with practical suggestions about how to address the central challenge of the time.

Fall down six times, get up seven.

Everybody talks about the need for resilience, the ability to bounce back from hardship, particularly in the current era of economic austerity. It is a popular concept. The need for inner resolve applies to school children as well as others at different ages and stages. If happiness is a mental state of being, then pupils should be able to control it through cognitive means. Positive thinking is not enough. False optimism sooner or later means disillusionment, anger and hopelessness.

At the opposite end of the well-being spectrum there are threatening consequences for a negative approach: pessimism is a reliable predictor of, and precursor to, damaging depression. We have a duty of care for our pupils and the need to develop systems that are fit for purpose has never been more pressing. In 2004 the Journal of Child Psychology and Psychiatry reported on a study comparing teenage mental health in 1974, 1986 and 1999. The report says, 'The mental health of teenagers has sharply declined in the last 25 years...the rate of emotional problems such as anxiety and depression has increased by 70% in adolescents'

I would like to suggest that the well-being agenda is not some idle, academic speculation or fantasy, the province of some cultist worldview or whimsical Pollyanna side track. There is a real mental health emergency in twenty-first century Britain, often under-reported and untreated. This is not only located in the western world but can be seen as a global epidemic.

What is more, the traditional defences against anxiety and depression, a hedonistic lifestyle of wealth and riches, is not a soft inoculation against the realities of the modern world and do not provide a panacea or guarantee in themselves of any sense of well-being. As I write, there is a sense of shock at the news of the death of high profile singer, Amy Winehouse. Winehouse joins the pantheon of her heroes - Kurt Cobain, Jimi Hendrix, Janis Joplin and Jim Morrison - all of whom died aged just 27. This begs one question, among many, about whether the education system could have in any way developed a better sense of resilience in these individuals, in order to deal with the extraordinary pressures they faced through their public personas? Or could an effective mentor or coach in later life have helped them find greater emotional equilibrium?

The mental health of adolescents remains a major cause of concern for those in educational circles who are charged with the responsibility for their emotional well-being. Today's school population are ten times more likely than their grandparents to suffer depression, the reason being that our culture has encouraged people to think about themselves more than they think about others. Stimulated by endless advertisements that offer overwhelming choices, our pupils sense of internal worth becomes linked to his or her degree of consumption. At the same time, the sense of community and commonality is rapidly shrinking out of sight.

Depending on our sources, current statistics suggest that 1 in 10 fourteen year olds are affected by depressive illness. Some suggest as many as 20%. Many more young people are suffering from high sub-clinical levels of depression that is under detected and under treated. Such depression often recurs and therefore children and adolescents are more likely to experience depression as adults.

The bad news for schools and families is that in children and adolescents, depression and high levels of anxiety symptoms are linked to poor academic achievement, interpersonal difficulties, behavioural problems, substance abuse, teenage pregnancy and in extreme cases, self-harm and death. Suicide among young people — defined as the 15-24 age group — is becoming increasingly common. It is more often a cause of death in young men than young women, and the ratio of male to female is four to one. Conversely, suicide attempts in all age groups are more common in females. Consider the case of Natasha Randall 17, who had a large circle of friends and was studying childcare when, without any indication that she was unhappy, hanged herself in her bedroom in January 2008. Her death was the latest in at least seven apparent copycat suicides in Bridgend, South Wales, that have alarmed parents, health authorities and police, who believe that they may have been prompted by messages on social networking websites.

Within days, two 15-year-old girls, both of whom had known Tasha, as she called herself, had also tried to take their lives. One cut her wrists and was later discharged from hospital into the care of her parents. The other tried to hang herself and spent two days on life support before showing signs of recovery. Police have visited the families of 20 of Tasha's friends, urging them to keep an eye on their daughters.

In the 12 months before Miss Randall's death, six young men from Bridgend and the surrounding area had killed themselves. Most were known to each other. She had attended the funeral of 20-year-old Liam Clarke, who was found, hanged in a local park the day after Boxing Day in 2007. This extraordinary litany of events beggars belief, and those of us in education are left wondering about the nature and dimensions of such powerful forces in youth culture that would lead to such a wasteful and distressing loss of life.

My thoughts are inextricably drawn at this point to the experience of a colleague in London and the tragic loss of his daughter, an exceptional student found dead at the foot of cliffs on the eve of leaving home for Oxford University. Angela, as we shall call her, 18, was due to start a chemistry degree course at New College, Oxford, after gaining four grade A's in her A levels. With everything to live for she drowned in the sea near Beachy Head, East Sussex, leaving her motive a mystery. Her parents were both successful school teachers and her home life appeared to have been happy. She was described as having an optimistic personality and as being someone who looked forward to life. She had a regular boyfriend with whom she had an excellent relationship. Angela had been deputy head girl. She had recently won the school's Cup for academic excellence and had excelled at her GCSEs, gaining 11 A* grades. She was reported missing from her home after being seen by her mother packing her cases. Her Toyota Carina car was found 20 miles away from her home at the top of the cliffs near Beachy Head, where she and her family had enjoyed walking. After she had disappeared, a search of the beach was made by coastguards and police, and her body was found at the foot of 175ft (53m) cliffs. The inquest at her death was told that there was uncertainty about how her body had sustained rib injuries. They could have been caused by a fall from the cliffs or from being buffeted about in the sea after she drowned.

In terms of Government tick boxes that mark highly desirable pupil achievement, Angela scored highly on any measure you care to mention. There was no history of family discord, rows or unfortunate incidents that are better forgotten and might provide embarrassment later. As captain of her school's hockey club, she led the team to victory in the regional Schoolgirls' Hockey Championships in 2001. She also played the oboe, appeared in school plays and was close to finishing her Duke of Edinburgh Gold Award.

Without knowing the full history, it is impossible to speculate on the causes of suicide but examinations, change of place of education or a house move, loss of friends or fear of loss of a boyfriend or girlfriend are all occasional motivating factors for it. Yet could it be also true that the education system that had seemly done so much might have potentially done more to help with the inner turmoil that led to this desperately sad and shockingly premature end? My motivation for writing this book is, in part, an effort to acknowledge the lives of these lost young people whose lives are too sad for diagnosis. There is a huge sense of grief. Someone has to learn from their mistakes, and pretty quickly if there is to be any way, at all, of preventing history from repeating itself, even if the outlook of only one young person can be changed. This in itself will make the effort all worthwhile.

As teachers in schools we need to be building capacities. We must not lower our expectations because of a false notion that high expectations logically leads to failure.

We need to rediscover the old truth that the secret of success is a combination of optimism, passion and the old-fashioned concept of hard work. For this there is no substitute, for it is true to say that we have become a nation that takes too many short cuts to happiness through pandering to our pleasure principles of mindless TV, retail therapy, drug and alcohol abuse, and self-medication through comfort food.

The good news is that finally, after a century of psychological study into emotional pathology (anxiety, depression, and obsession) direct evidence about the ambiguous relationship between material and subjective well-being has been generated, after a long moratorium during which studies on happiness were considered too soft for scientists to undertake.

Children need to adapt to their difficulties by dealing effectively with the challenges of modern life. Unashamedly we need to offer to children at school, and in the home, building blocks for the future including:

- The capacity for optimism, earthed in the reality of modern life, but nevertheless buoyed by the belief that things can work out for the good.
- The nurturing of faith and a sense of meaning something to make life purposeful.
- Fostering a pre dilection for helping others, engendering the pro-social behaviour of giving generously and joyously.
- Helping to focus on strengths, what the children can know, understand and do rather than applying negative labels, dressed up in the spurious language of mix and match computer phraseology that currently serves as school assessments and reports.
- We need to encourage the children to develop the ability to set goals, and provide suitable role models, either from contemporary examples or from history.
- We need to provide appropriate social support when the necessary social capital is missing.

These practical suggestions, if enacted through a group of teachers who work hard to establish firm but fair relationships with their pupils, will undoubtedly build the necessary capacity to help children bounce back when they face difficulties.

The aim of good schools is to catalyze a change in our educational psychology and practice from a pre-occupation with the pathology of repairing the worst behaviours and performers and also to build the best qualities in life for the majority.

A straight forward way of viewing the problem is to say that **happiness is not to be found in the negation of unhappiness**. Whilst it is still possible to study the antecedents for anxiety, neurosis, anger, depression, psychosis in a growing number of adolescents, what we need to do also, particularly in schools, is to **actively study ways of pursuing well-being, satisfaction, joy, excitement and happiness**. Improved physical health is just one of the potential benefits of optimism that is being discussed here. While evidence that it may increase our resistance to physiological disease remains ambiguous, there is little question that a child who has learned to be more optimistic and employs the various techniques promoted by Positive Psychology (from developing gratitude and practising mindfulness, to making it a point to nurture social relationships with friends and family) will be less likely to succumb to psychological illnesses, such as depression and anxiety. Thus, cultivating happiness - more than just an end in itself - also acts as a psychological buffer, creating resistance to numerous specific mental disorders. Perhaps this does not provide an outright inoculation against anxiety and depression, but a healthy resistance, nonetheless - something no rational parent would want to deny to their children.

Taking an example from other professions, preventative medicine is as important in educational psychology as it is in physical healthcare. Through my research, I have found out that there is substance in the work of psychologists such as Marty Seligman when they say that are human strengths that can act as buffers against mental illness: courage, future-mindedness, optimism, interpersonal skill, faith, work ethic, hope, honesty, perseverance, the capacity for flow and insight, to name several. It is possible to demonstrate empirically that cultivating and learning optimism prevents depression and anxiety in children and adults, roughly halving their incidence over the next two years.

The message of Seligman and his colleagues is to remind those of us in education that the psychology of education is not just about the province of failure, misbehaviour and damage just because certain individuals shout the loudest for our attention. It also is the study of strength and virtue, building what is right. Educational psychology should not be just about the domains of underperformance, dyslexia and dyspraxia; it should also be about what works, insights about success and strengths, love, growth, and play. In this quest for what is best, a positivistic psychology does not rely on wishful thinking or self-deceit. Rather, it tries to adapt what is best in the scientific method to the unique problems that human behaviour presents in all its complexity.

We need to focus on transformation as opposed to mere information. The assumption that has to be made clear right from the start is that it is reasonable to want to be happier as well as achieve a greater sense of well-being: neuroscience can easily support this notion. In the last century it was thought that human intelligence and our potential for feelings of happiness had a set point. Now it is suggested that modern neuroscience has propagated theories of brain elasticity and that the cortex is far more malleable. New neural pathways and connections will allow new actions, choices and behaviours, thus impacting on our emotional state. Long-lasting adjustments can be made to our levels of well-being and happiness.

At the heart of this humanistic, positivistic theory is the premise that it can become possible to appreciate beauty, be more appreciative of the past, mindful of the present and optimistic for the future in new ways that will become part of a self-reinforcing cycle that will have meaning for our lives. This is more difficult in the modern world where we no longer have easily available the models for attractive lives, the great variety of craftsmen, the up-right citizens, those with saintly natures or patriots who can show us the better way.

Today the celebrity culture is a more vivid and immediate influence on pupil aspiration. Developing character traits over time seems less appetizing to children than the seduction of overnight success, as witnessed on X factor. The very notion of describing character traits may be considered inappropriate for their prescriptive, morally laden nature. We prefer to use personality as a lighter, more politically correct descriptor. So I think it is true to say that we tend to prefer to embrace self-esteem, physical attractiveness, assertiveness, autonomy, wealth and competitiveness as desirable physical and personality traits as opposed to the ubiquitous personal characteristics and virtues identified by the positive psychologists (namely wisdom, courage, love and humanity, justice, temperance and spirituality) that act as a more authoritative classification and measurement of human strengths.

The good news is that change for the better is possible: we are not immutably shaped by genes or inextricably constrained by the environments in which we live. We ourselves and the children that we teach can be the new role models, the new agents of social change that society so desperately needs. This will not be by force of will or by making New Year's resolutions.

I am so grateful to Marty Seligman for reminding us, through his theories, of the fallacy that our past determines our future, a motivation that can end in passivity or learned hopelessness. He cites how the prevailing psycho-social orthodoxies of Darwin, Marx and Freud have imprisoned us for too long. What we come to do in the future does not have to be a determined product laid down by our ancestors. Recent history has demythologized the inevitability of the collapse of capitalism. We are not determined by our resolution of sexual and aggressive conflicts, a fallacy espoused by Freud.

Indeed, the data around my own childhood demonstrate that the events of childhood are inaccurate predictors of the future. Some empirical data exists to support the theory of destructive effects of negative childhood on adult development – the loss of a mother before eleven is one, and a parents' divorce has slight disruptive effect on later adolescence. Seligman (2002, p.67) suggests that problems wane as we grow up and are not easily detectable in adulthood. He should know – he has spent decades studying the minutiae of these effects.

We would all like to know the short cuts to happiness if such a list existed. We need to know first, what the constituents of happiness look like. Positive Psychology demonstrates that this can easily be expressed as a simple, commonsense formula:

$H = S + C + V$.

The level of happiness that we actually encounter (H) is determined by our biological set point (S) plus the conditions of our life (C) plus the voluntary activities that we engage in (V).

I am naturally cynical about quick fixes, short cuts, lifeless long lists and snake oil salesmen but this little formula does enough to quieten the scrutiny of my inner lawyer that serves to alert me to fraud of any sort. One important part of the work of teachers in this is to find out what conditions in schools (education as happiness) and activities (education for happiness) can push pupil well-being to the top of its potential range.

This leads me to the happy conclusion that the defeatist 'promissory note' that Freud wrote about childhood events determining the course of our adult lives is as valuable as a share in the bank of Bernard Madoff. The underlying imprisoning ideology of Darwin and Freud have been so entrenched in austerity Britain that many reading these words may well be still constrained by feelings of embitterness about the past and a sense of passivity about shaping future events. The concept of Positive Psychology can lead to a new, liberating realization that we are not being co-erced to a future dictated by childhood events. If we look carefully there will be enough to celebrate and appreciate in our own biographies. This appreciation will, in turn, promote a greater sense of contentment and serenity.

No one in the UK is of necessity, doomed to misery strictly because of their environmental circumstances. Talking straight, no matter what happens to us, we are always in control over how we perceive, interpret and react to our circumstances - see Victor Frankl's 'Man's Search for Meaning'. This classic could be described as one of the most important popular books of the 20th century. It has an extraordinary message about the meaning of life and its psychological importance. As a psychiatrist, Frankl emphasized that having a purpose, both in the short-term as well as in 'big picture' terms, is essential to mental health, resilience and life satisfaction. He is himself an example of his theory in action and says much to support a world view that advocates a positive, psychological approach.

Frankl's own personal experience demonstrates that even living through the horrors of a concentration camp during The Holocaust does not destroy all hope of living a satisfying, meaningful life. Reading that a man can be content and fulfilled, even 'happy,' in the face of having lived through the wretched conditions and daily atrocities of Auschwitz (and three other concentration camps) and the murder of his wife and both parents, most people are stunned into disbelief, but ultimately come away with hope and inspiration.

This does not mean to say we should do nothing - just because a man is able to survive and thrive in the face of oppressive conditions does not justify tolerating or even promoting these conditions. Though Frankl led a satisfying, happy life, by no means does he condone or encourage opening concentration camps. Science can - and should - try to explain adequately even the worst of human behaviour, but such explanations are never justifications.

Plato wrote that the most urgent task for educators is to teach young people to find pleasure in the right things. A pre requisite for happiness is the ability to get fully involved in life. Classes in well-being supported and underpinned by strong empirical evidence, can help to achieve this ideal. Not everything in life is a zero-sum game. This is a beautiful example of a win-win situation: not only will our pupils be happier, but also healthier. We can all agree that this is a good thing.

Chapter 3: The rationale for pupil well-being lessons

The entitlement to education has been established as a basic human right: since1952, Article 2 of the first Protocol to the European Convention on Human Rights obliges all signatory parties to guarantee the right to education. At a world level, the United Nations' International Covenant on Economic, Social and Cultural Rights of 1966 guarantees this right under its Article 13. What is not stipulated are the nature and dimensions of this entitlement.

Having demonstrated in the previous chapter that pupil well-being should be taken seriously, one fundamental task would be to investigate further whether the well-being of pupils is a **purpose** or a **function** of the educational process. It is worth making a distinction between the two. A purpose can be described as the direct goal of the process, a focused target or end to be achieved. Functions, in contrast, are other outcomes that may occur as a natural result of the process as by-products or consequences.

Some maintain that the transmission of core knowledge is the central purpose of education, while the transfer of such knowledge from school to the individual's experience of the wider world is something that happens naturally as a consequence of possessing that knowledge, a function of education. It can be argued that because purposes can be construed as an expressed goal, more effort is put into attaining it. As Peters reminds us (1986), 'What gets measured, gets done.' This is particularly pertinent in the United Kingdom where schools' purposes, expressed as aims, become the benchmark by which they are measured by the Inspectorate of the office for Standards in Education. Functions, by contrast, are assumed to occur without directed effort.

The ambivalence about purposes and function is problematic for teachers who are presented with a wide range of possible directions and priorities, with no clear direction other than the imperative to improve their standing in government league table based on exam results. I say that there is no better purpose for a school than for the teachers to make a massive contribution to a pupil's well-being by giving him or her sense of gratitude and appreciation, plus promoting a character trait of resilience and optimism for life in the future.

The transmission of information, in itself, can never be enough. Much information is thrown at pupils from all quarters through new information highways, most of the time to little effect. Instead, our schools should be places of **transformation** not mere information. Information on its own will not change the world. Surely we should be uncovering human potential to encourage our pupils. In Maslow's words the function of education, the goal of education, the human goal, the humanistic goal, the goal so far as human beings are concerned, is ultimately the 'self-actualization of a person, the becoming fully human, the development of the fullest height that the human species can stand up to or that the particular individual can come to. In a less technical way, it is helping the person to become the best that he is able to become.To achieve this aspirational, transformational model will require twenty first century schools to support a curriculum that is much more concerned with the softer interpersonal and intrapersonal skills than they are prepared to commit to at present. It will require brave decisions by policy makers and those who are currently fixated by a league table mentality, for whom pupils are mere statistic in terms of their attainment of GCSE's at grades A* to C

Purposes or functions? A model for a broad curriculum (Lee 2012)

MORAL DEVELOPMENT: acquisition /clarification of personal values	**DISCERNMENT:** ability to recognize and evaluate different points of view	**INTEGRITY:** ability to live a fulfilling life
SOCIABILITY: formation of healthy relationships between pupils and teachers	**SUSTAINABILITY:** cultivating an ecological understanding	**INTRA-PERSONAL:** self-esteem, self-reflection, self-awareness, self-realization
KNOWLEDGE ACQUISITION: acquiring knowledge about the past and present	**DECISION MAKING:** capacity to evaluate information and to predict future outcomes.	**CREATIVITY:** capacity to think creatively.
PHYSICAL: motor skills, hand eye co-ordination.	**WELL-BEING /HAPPINESS:** mental and physical health	**INTER-PERSONAl:** understanding human relations and motivations
PROBLEM-SOLVING: capacity to seek out alternative solutions and evaluate them	**COGNITIVE DEVELOPMENT:** developing skills of analysis, synthesis, evaluation	**CITIZENSHIP:** knowledge of ethical standards acceptable by society and the capacity
UTILITY: capacity to earn a living: career education	**COMMUNICATION:** writing, speaking, listening	

My current viewpoint is that this is, in fact, what wider society requires and what industry demands. The challenges are to change an established yet inefficient, ineffective education service in austerity Britain, to break established orthodoxies and establish new innovations, such as making the well-being of pupils a central purpose of modern schooling. In a survey of 1,137 employers in 2008, while good literacy and numeracy were said to be critical, equally important were enthusiasm, commitment and timekeeping. For occupational attainment, non-cognitive traits are as important overall as cognitive skills. This has been demonstrated on many occasions when I have questioned key business leaders directly, for example at the Goldman Sachs' headquarters (2009) in London and the top leadership team at Novartis in Basel (2010 and 2011). The common theme seemed to suggest almost a reversal of prevailing orthodoxy that the hard skills of literacy and numeracy should maintain their almost unassailable position at the top of the curricular hierarchy.

Could it be that our fundamental beliefs about the purpose and function of education have been blurred in the race for league table results? Teaching children is not merely about correcting their epistemological shortcomings. They can work hard towards doing those themselves with our expertise and help. Our purpose is to nurture their strengths - their social intelligences - and help them find a sense of well-being by shaping their lives around these strengths. These would buffer their less developed areas against the potential tyranny of circumstances. There will be huge societal benefits if we can re-engineer the situation to put people in places where their strengths find their full expression. For 90% of all teenagers, the best psychology is not one that is central focused on pathology – this is not applicable. We need to be asking how pupils can find happiness and optimism, competence, mastery as we pursue better paths for good and meaningful lives.

Thus this book is a call to action for school leaders to revisit their mission, vision and values. Notwithstanding the hollow rhetoric about the development of all aspects of the educational experience provided for pupils contained in many school promotional web-sites, prospectuses and mission statements, it can be argued that it is the statistically measurable content of assessments that is one of the principal drivers of education currently in the UK. This places school leaders who hold a broader view of the purpose of education in a dilemma: the purpose they assign to education is often at variance to the meaning assigned by other members of their communities. After many years of central government obsession with testing, there is a strong desire in many for more freedom from centralized bureaucracies.

On an anecdotal level, as a Headteacher of twenty years standing, when I ask any prospective parents at my school what it is their desire for their children, they always reply 'happiness'. The definition of this catch-all term is perhaps not so easily attainable. Nevertheless, this sentiment is reflected throughout society. In the words of the Dali Lama, whether one believes in religion or not, whether one believes in this religion or that religion, the very purpose of our life is happiness, the very motion of our life is towards happiness. Similarly, William James proposes that if we were to ask the question: 'What is human life's chief concern?' one of the answers we should receive would be: 'It is happiness.' How to gain, how to keep, how to recover happiness, is in fact for most men at all times the secret motive of all they do, and of all they are willing to endure. How schools are purposive in their activity to support these vital aims remained unclear and vague up to this point.

In addition to personal experience, there is also very good research evidence to support the benefits of a broader view about the purposes of education other than a sterile, functionalist rationale. McLaughlin and Clarke (2010) state that 'schools should be involved in developing emotional well-being' and that, as Resnick (2005) has written, this involves 'the intentional, deliberative process of providing support, relationships, experience and opportunities that promote positive outcomes for young people'.

CONNECTED UNDERSTANDING :
FIVE JUSTIFICATIONS FOR PROMOTING PUPIL WELL-BEING IN SCHOOLS

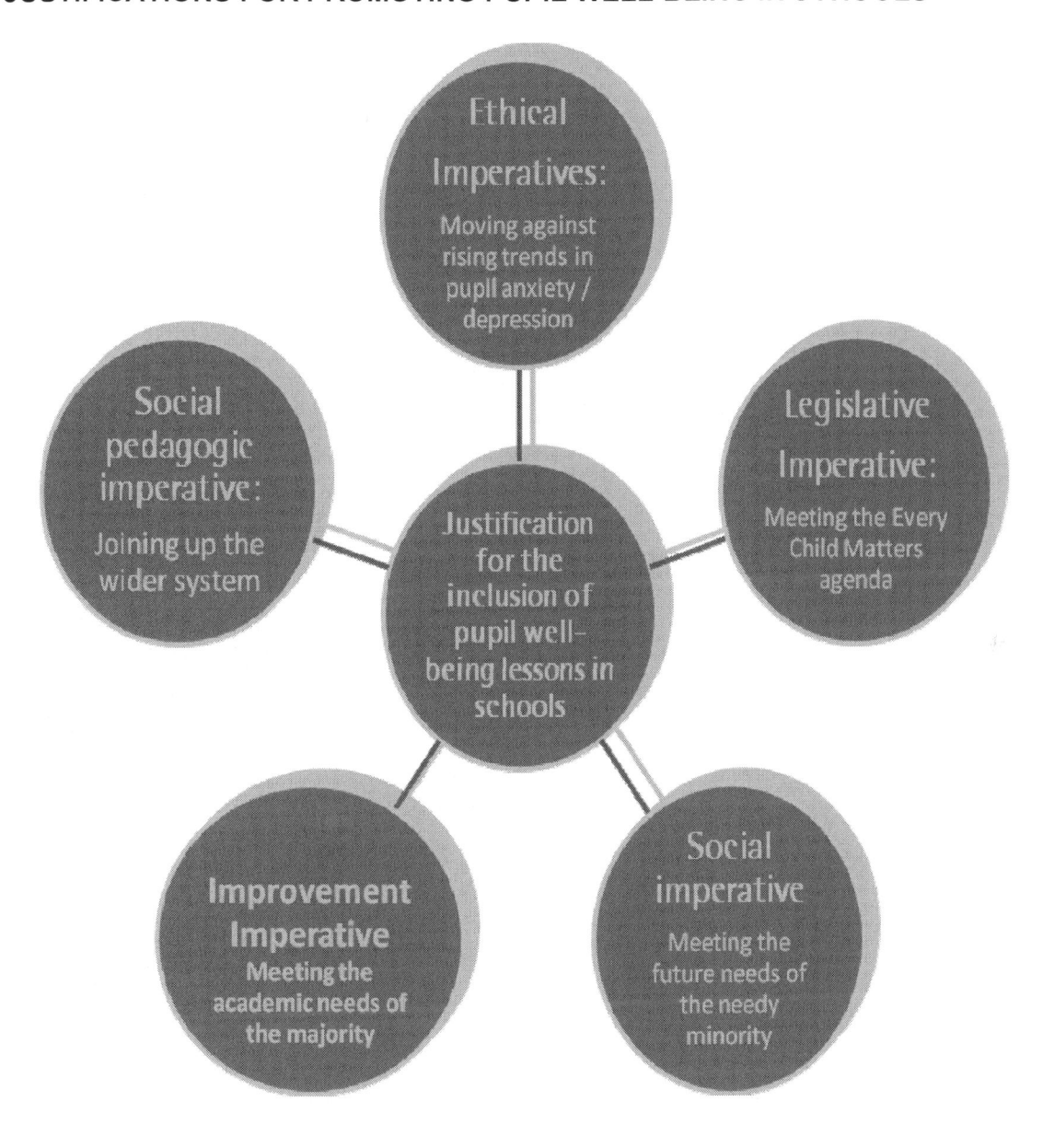

- **Ethical Imperatives:** Moving against rising trends in pupil anxiety / depression
- **Legislative Imperative:** Meeting the Every Child Matters agenda
- **Social imperative:** Meeting the future needs of the needy minority
- **Improvement Imperative:** Meeting the academic needs of the majority
- **Social pedagogic imperative:** Joining up the wider system

Justification for the inclusion of pupil well-being lessons in schools

Lee (2012)

An ethical Imperative

It vital to promote pupil well-being for a number of reasons. Firstly, if we can accurately assess mental health problems, and we know both how to intervene and also that intervention may work, then **there is an ethical imperative to lead improvement initiatives immediately** (Nuffield Foundation, 2004).

There are a number of different ways of assessing the general well-being of adolescents as a whole. These include measures of both behavioural and social indicators, and measures of happiness and life satisfaction. Adolescent mental health is one of these key indicators of well-being. Surveys suggest that clinically significant emotional or behavioural difficulties are restricted to a minority of around one in ten children aged 11-15 years, who show one or more of these problems at any given point in time. An important issue, though, is whether these types of difficulties are increasing. The Rutter and Smith study group showed that rises in adolescent mental health problems in the mid to late 20th century were 'surprising and troubling' (p.782) and occurred in nearly all developed countries. What we are seeing with new data (Collishaw et al 2004) is that the trend has continued upwards in the UK.

There is a wide range of possible causes for changes to the well-being of adolescents, and while few if any have been properly researched, most have been raised somewhere in the research literature, albeit in a rather tentative way. The key point is that those who are supported and have more positive experiences can learn better and are more likely to fulfill their social and academic potential. It is likely that intervening more effectively and imaginatively could significantly reduce adolescent mortality (through reducing suicide rates) and improve life experiences.

The ability of a child to connect to school during adolescence has been shown to be a key protective factor and one that lowers the likelihood of health-risk behaviour, while also enhancing positive educational outcomes (Resnick et al, 199; Resnick, 2000; Glover et al, 1998; Blum and Libbey, 2004; Libbey, 2004 in McLaughlin and Clarke 2010).

The quality of early adolescents' relationship with school is instrumental to their social and cognitive development, leading to sense of achievement and high self-esteem, but it is also fundamental to their well-being (Finn, 1993; Newmann; 1992: Marks 2000).

Several factors relate to young adolescents' sense of motivation and achievement at school, including parental support (Bowen and Bowen, 1998; Rosenfeld et al, 2000) and peer support (Rosenfeld et al, 2000). Young adolescents who are disengaged from school, and have poor relationships with peers and teachers, are likely to have a higher risk of displaying anxiety or depressive symptoms, are more likely to use drugs and engage in socially disruptive behaviours, and are less likely to complete secondary schools (Resnick et al, 1997: Bond et al, 2004; Barclay and Doll, 2001; Doll and Hess, 2001; Marcus and Sanders-Reio, 2001; Catalano et al, 1996).

McLaughlin and Clarke (2010) develop the theme of connectedness through their careful review of the literature. To have a sense of connectedness with school, it is suggested that a child should feel that they belong in some way to the school (Finn 1993, 1997). Children who feel connected to school, and feel cared for by people at school, report a higher degree of well-being (Resnick et al, 1997; Eccles et al, 1997; Steinberg, 1996; McNeely et al, 2002). Smith (2006) in a study of youth transitions and crime in Edinburgh emphasizes the role of teacher-pupil relationships in this attachment to school.

> *Attachment to school is related to young people's behaviour more widely in school and more widely to delinquent and criminal conduct. The most important dimension is attachment to teachers, but the belief that school success will bring later reward is also important* (p.4).

Attachment to adults who care is at the centre of engagement with school and through the school with society. It suggests identification with social organizations though attachment.

A legislative Imperative

Secondly, in terms of the roles that schools and school leaders can play, it can be reasonably argued that there is a fundamental assumption in many policy programmes that schools can impact upon young people's well-being .Schemes such as the *Social and Emotional Aspects of Learning in Schools (SEAL)* (Dept. for Education and Skills 2005) suggest that teachers and schools have a part to play in developing young people's well-being.

Furthermore, the government's recent *Every Child Matters* legislation (Department for Education and Skills, 2003) places a duty of well-being on schools. A full suite of descriptors has been provided to enable inspectors and schools to pitch their judgments about how well pupils are doing across the range of outcomes. The revised Framework gives priority to promoting well-being and narrowing gaps: evaluating the achievement and well-being of pupils and assessing the extent to which schools ensure that all pupils, including those most at risk, succeed.

A social Imperative

Thirdly, in the longer-term, a significant proportion of young people with mental health problems will go on to be adults with not just ongoing mental health problems, but also a range of other poor outcomes as well – difficulties with relationships, unstable employment histories, involvement in crime, and social exclusion, care, and unemployment benefits, quite apart from the personal costs to the individual.

At the core of this argument is the notion that developing a holistic approach, where due regard is given to pupil well-being, should become a key aim for school leaders. McLaughlin and Clarke (2010) are right when they argue that schools are powerful institutions which influence social development and there is a need to have appropriate **social goals,** in contrast to a discourse of managing behaviour and a narrow focus on the 'academic', which views it as separate from the emotional and social. It is easy for the principal purpose of schools to be centred on knowledge transmission and teaching rather than to embrace the broader needs of the learner. In turn, pupils are expected to conform to the process of school rather than schools serving the needs of their pupils.

A school improvement Imperative

Fourthly, a careful consideration of statistics proves that the majority of students have different needs other than the prevention of depression. At any point in time, approximately 2% of children aged 11-15 and 11% of youth aged 16-24 in Great Britain have a major depressive disorder (Green et al 2005; Singleton, Bumpstead et al, 2001)', quoted in Karen Reivich et al, the Penn Resiliency Project Executive Summary, March 2009): this of course leaves 98% and 89% of 11-15 and 16-24 year olds respectively *without* major depressive disorders. There is further research evidence available to suggest that when education for well-being retains an appropriate place within the curriculum, there are broad benefits for all pupils. Understanding well-being will enhance academic learning.

A socio-pedagogic Imperative

Fifthly, although well-being is not merely the province of specialist class teaching in schools it is a pivotal task in wider, whole curricular and systemic activities e.g. The Healthy Schools Programme (NHSP) is a joint initiative between DCSF and Department of Health (DH) which promotes a whole school / whole child approach to health. The Programme has existed since 1999. It is recognised as a key delivery mechanism in the Children's Plan (DCSF, 2007) and in Healthy Weight, Healthy Lives (Department of Health 2008).

The Healthy Schools Programme is intended to deliver real benefits in respect of:

- Improvement in health and reduced health inequalities;
- Raised pupil achievement;
- More social inclusion; and,
- Closer working between health promotion providers and education establishments

Pupil well-being has thus become a national concern, reflected by provision in extended services and could play a key role in any attempt to introduce a broader social pedagogy. It reflects a desire for all children and young people to be healthy and achieve at school and in life. In the longer term, this will lead to improved health, reduced health inequalities, increased social inclusion and raise achievement for all. Education for well-being could have important school improvement outcomes in terms of pupil attainment, behaviour, satisfaction, future life chances, resilience and creativity (Ennals 2009).

The situation described is thus very complex, both in causes and in solutions. This book is purposely set within the broader field of 'well-being' to indicate that it is a part of a much bigger picture that should draw in the promotion of positive health as well as measurement of symptoms. It is here that a positive psychological approach, espoused by Martin Seligman, Daniel Goleman, Richard Layard and more indirectly Howard Gardner, can provide a framework as part of the growing literature on happiness and pupil well-being.
The field's steering committee includes a number of psychologists and psychiatrists who have done highly regarded clinical work: Ed Diener of the University of Illinois at Urbana-Champaign, whose specialty is 'subjective well-being'; Christopher Peterson at the University

of Michigan, who has made a study of admired character traits around the world; George Vaillant, who has long headed a Harvard project tracking success and failure among the college's graduates; and Mihaly Csikszentmihalyi of Claremont Graduate University, who has spent years studying 'optimal functioning,' or the state of being intensely absorbed in a task, what he calls 'flow.' This concept describes an experience that is so enjoyable and engrossing that it is worth doing for its own sake. Creative activities in sport and music are typical sources for these autotelic experiences. The common characteristics of this kind of experience are

1. You know very clearly what has to be done moment by moment because the activity requires it or because goals are set along each step.

2. There is immediate feedback on what is being done. – the activity might provide information or the person has an internalized standard.

3. There is a feeling that the person has an ability to match the opportunities for action. When challenges are in balance with skills, one becomes lost in the activity and flow is likely to result. If challenges are too great for skill levels, then anxiety is the likely product. If skills are greater than the challenge, the result is boredom.

This description of activities requires skills, concentration and perseverance. The relationship between flow and happiness is not entirely obvious – people don't normally reflect on their emotional state during flow as they are so engrossed. When the flow or optimal experience is over, people report having been in as positive state as it is possible to feel.

At this stage, it will be useful to understand the antecedents and development of the positive psychological approach.

Chapter 4: Background to the positive psychological approach

The key assumption of this book is that we all have a self-organizing capacity to achieve a positive internal state without having to rely exclusively on a pharmacological solution. A number of contemporary psychologists have demonstrated quite convincingly that cognitive techniques can help restructure an individual's goals and improve their quality of life. These include

- Maslow's self-actualization theory (1968,1971)
- Block and Block's ego resilience (1980)
- Diener's positive emotionality, (1984)
- Antonovsky's salutogenic approach (1979)
- Seeman's personality integration (1996)
- Ryan and Deci's autonomy (1985)
- Csikszentmihalyi's optimal psychological states or 'flow' (1999)
- Scheier and Carver's dispositional optimism (198) and
- Seligman's learned optimism(1991)

Positive Psychology is the scientific study of optimal human functioning, focusing on factors that allow individuals and communities to thrive. In short, Positive Psychology is the science of happiness and well-being.

Prof. Martin Seligman, former Chair of the American Psychological Association and a widely recognized founder of the Positive Psychology approach, argues that American psychology before World War II had three objectives:

1. to cure mental illness,
2. to make relatively untroubled people happier
3. to study genius and high talent (Seligman 1993).

Seligman argues that psychology since World War II has reduced its scope to repairing weakness and understanding suffering. It is possible to recognize considerable advancements e.g. a classification of mental illness has been devised that allows international collaboration, and through this collaboration, effective psychotherapeutic or pharmacological treatments for 14 major mental disorders have been developed.

Positive Psychology brings the same attention to positive emotions (happiness, pleasure, and well-being) that clinical psychology has always paid to the negative ones (depression, anger, resentment). Psychoanalysis once promised to turn acute human misery into ordinary suffering; Positive Psychology promises to take mild human pleasure and turn it into a profound state of well-being.

Whilst modern psychologists have built a strong science and practice of treating mental illness, Seligman maintains that everyday well-being has been largely ignored. This could be because of a faulty supposition that the absence of mental illness and suffering is sufficient to let individuals and communities flourish. There is good evidence to indicate that the absence of illness does not constitute happiness (Diener & Lucas 2000). Those committed to a science of Positive Psychology can draw on the effective research methods developed to understand and treat mental illness. Results from a randomized, placebo-controlled study demonstrate that people are happier and less depressed three months after completing exercises targeting positive emotion (Seligman, 1993).

The ultimate goal of Positive Psychology is to make people happier by understanding and building positive emotion, gratification and meaning (Seligman 2002). Such affirmations of self-worth are empty without concurrent success in the world. The feeling of self-esteem is a by-product of doing well. It cannot be separated from action. Towards this end, those working in schools and in families must supplement what we know about how to address illness and repairing damage with knowledge about nurturing well-being in individuals and school communities. It is time to turn our concentration away from a default model that focuses on psychopathologies in our pedagogy to concentrate on the study of strengths and virtues. We should work towards developing interventions that can help people become
lastingly happier.

Seligman writes that we have also been misled in believing that feeling good about ourselves can come about through trying to avoid 'bad' feelings. In fact, this avoidance can itself lead to depression. Feeling anger, sadness and anxiety can be useful as indicators of the need for change and as a driving force towards mastery and action. It is necessary to fail, feel bad and to try again repeatedly until success occurs. When we impulsively protect our children from failure, we deprive them of learning mastery skills.

It can be suggested that even if we were successful at removing depression, anxiety and anger, that would not result in happiness. The argument here is that 'happiness' is a condition over and above the absence of unhappiness. That said, there is very little in the educational research literature about how to improve the lives of the pupils whose days are largely free of overt mental dysfunction but are potentially bereft of pleasure, engagement and meaning. We did not know much up to this point about how we can construct a programme that makes pupils optimistic, caring, generous, content, engaged, or creative. We now have clearer ideas about how to promote a sense of optimism. In sum, whether you are a pessimist or an optimist depends on how you explain bad events to yourself. Our mother and teachers had the most influence on our 'explanatory style.' This puts a great deal of responsibility on teachers to get this right. Through effective teaching, it is possible to change our 'explanatory style' to be more optimistic.

A pessimistic world view creates a downward emotional spiral: pessimists often personalize bad events, attributing them to permanent, pervasive causes. Yet they ascribe temporary, impersonal, specific causes to good events. The projection of present despair into the future causes hopelessness.

By contrast, teachers should encourage in their pupils the ability to externalize adversity's causes and see them as fleeting and specific, and to credit good events to personal, permanent, pervasive causes. With this optimistic outlook, pupils will be much quicker to get over a setback and try again.

Defining well-being and happiness

Things won are done; joy's soul lies in the doing.

-William Shakespeare, *Troilus and Cressida, Act 1, Scene 2*

Today, in the author's experience as a leader in four London schools for over a twenty-five year period, when parents are asked directly about the purpose of school they inevitably talk in terms of the school making a positive impact on their child's happiness. It is not always clear how they would define such happiness or whether that might be achieved through their child's advancement over others. The quest for happiness or 'well-being' is not a new phenomenon. What is unclear is the direct role of the school in achieving this purpose. Thus our first concern is to determine what it is we are trying to increase in schools.

Some see a limited value in discussing a somewhat vague notion of happiness and prefer instead to embrace a compound noun '*well-being*'. The two terms have tended to be interchangeable.

The Foresight Report, published by the Government Office for Science in 2008 defines well-being as follows:

> 'Well-being is a dynamic state, in which the individual is able to develop their potential, work productively and creatively, build strong and positive relationships with others, and contribute to their community.'

Other words that are often associated with well-being are 'flourishing', 'thriving' and the Greek word *eudemonia*, which Aristotle used to denote happiness, or 'the worthwhile life.'

What is happiness and can happiness / well-being be taught? Science cannot presume to answer these questions but can highlight components of happiness and investigate empirically what builds those components. A review of the literature leads to three possible constituents of happiness.

Within limits, we can increase:

- our positive emotion about the **past (by cultivating gratitude and forgiveness)**
- our positive emotion about the **present (by savouring and mindfulness)**
- our positive emotion about the **future (by building hope and optimism)**.

Positive Emotions

The **first route** to greater happiness is **hedonic**, increasing positive emotion. Beyond pleasure and optimism, all aspects of happiness are explored in Positive Psychology, from rapture and ecstasy, to contentment and satisfaction. We are learning more and more about positive emotions as they relate to the past, present and future; gratitude, joy, and hope being just one example of each.

In addition to researching transient hedonic sensations, more attention is being shifted to what is known to be a source of lasting, authentic happiness - the pursuit of 'the pleasant life', 'the good life', and 'the meaningful life', each generating more genuine contentment than the last.

Unlike the other two routes to happiness, the route relying on positive emotions has clear limits. Positive affectivity is heritable, and our emotions fluctuate within a genetically determined range. It is worthwhile to increase the amount of positive emotion in our lives, but we can boost our hedonics only so high. When people fluctuate within a relatively 'down' range of positive emotion, but live in a society that promotes an upbeat disposition, they can feel discouraged and even defective.

Drawing on character strengths

Positive emotion is not the sole determinant of happiness and well-being, and it is possible to offer a broader conception of happiness than mere hedonics (Seligman, 2002).

A **second route** to happiness involves the pursuit of '**gratification**'. The key characteristic of a gratification is that it engages us fully. Although there are shortcuts to pleasures, no shortcuts exist to gratification. Seligman argues that the pursuit of gratifications requires us to draw on character strengths such as creativity, social intelligence, sense of humour, perseverance, and an appreciation of beauty and excellence. Gratifications are not necessarily accompanied by positive emotions. Indeed, the pursuit of a gratification may be, at times, unpleasant e.g. endurance events. Finding flow in gratifications need not involve anything larger than the self.

Serving something higher

A **third route** to happiness comes from **using individual strengths to belong to and in the service of something larger than ourselves:** something such as knowledge, goodness, family, community, politics, justice or a higher spiritual power. The third route gives life meaning.

The Psychology of happiness: towards a 'full life'.

1. Positive Emotion
'the pleasant life'

2. Engagement
'the good life'

3. Meaning
'the meaningful life'

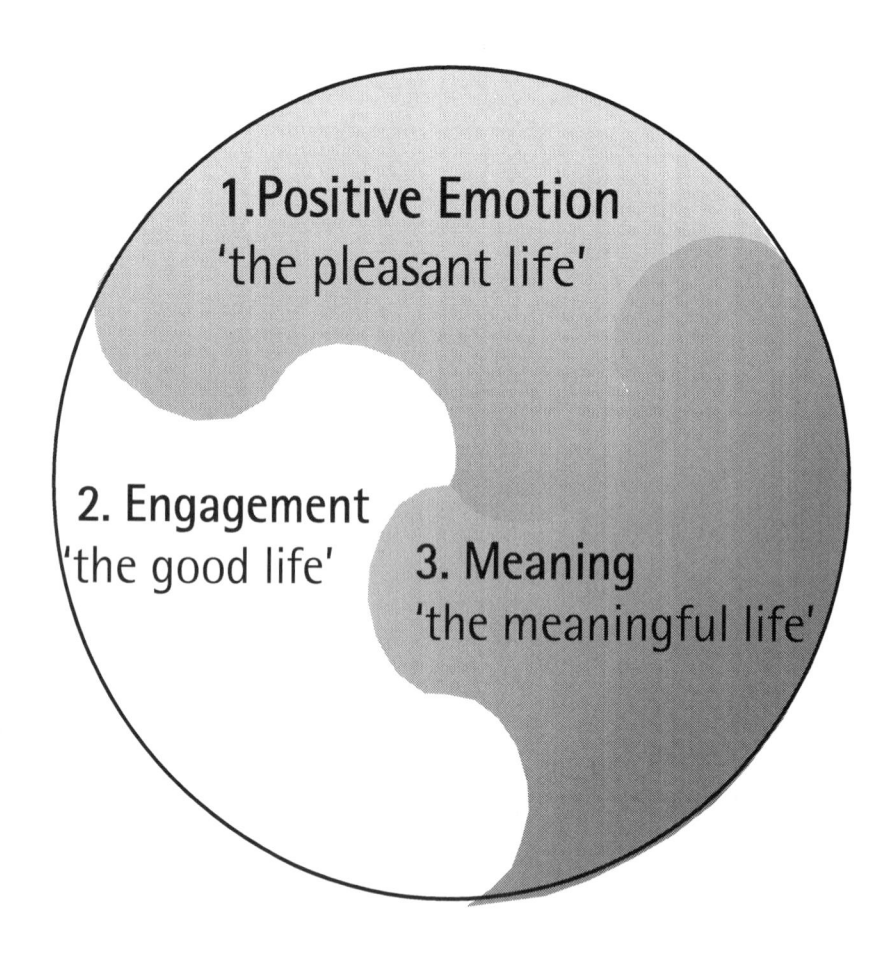

Peterson et al (2005) develop reliable measures for all three routes to happiness and demonstrate that people differ in their tendency to rely on one rather than another.

   a. We call a tendency to pursue happiness by boosting positive emotion, 'the pleasant life'
   b. The tendency to pursue happiness via the gratifications, 'the good life';
   c. The tendency to pursue happiness via using our strengths towards something larger than ourselves, 'the meaningful life'.

A person who uses all three routes to happiness leads the 'full life', and recent empirical evidence suggests that those who lead the full life have much the greater life satisfaction (Peterson et al. 2005).

Flourishing – a new well-being theory.

Since the conclusion of Seligman's critically acclaimed thesis 'Authentic Happiness' in 2002, he has published a new book (2011) that develops this happiness formula, to create an all-encompassing well-being theory. This has been achieved by adding two elements, namely:

Relationships: positive relationships (or their absence), it is argued, have a profound impact on an individual's well-being. It is difficult to decide whether positive relationships should be pursued for their own sake or because they bring positive emotion, meaning, accomplishment or engagement.

Achievement.: Seligman argues that achievement is a distinguishable and fundamental element of well-being. Motivation is not merely a case of drive reduction but can be seen as the way in which people act to exert mastery over challenges or the environment.

The most recent research then, suggests that well-being has five inter-dependable elements:

The Psychology Of Wellbeing
The PERMA Model Of Wellbeing [Seligman 2011]

Relationships — Positive emotion — Achievement — Engagement — Meaning — Wellbeing

Positive emotion about the past: the link between Gratitude and Well-being

Given the importance of the quality of interpersonal relationships in schools and families, gratitude inspires pro-social reciprocity and indeed, is one of the primary psychological mechanisms thought to underlie reciprocal altruism. This means that the experience of gratitude, and the actions stimulated by it, build and strengthen social bonds and friendships. A grateful response to life circumstances may be an adaptive psychological strategy and an important process by which people positively interpret everyday experiences. The ability to notice, appreciate, and savor the elements of one's life has been viewed as a crucial determinant of well-being.

Fredrickson's (1998, 2000) broaden-and-build model of positive emotions may be especially helpful here. She has argued that positive emotions broaden mindsets and build enduring personal resources (Fredrickson, 1998). These resources function as reserves to be drawn on in times of need. Seen in the light of this model, gratitude is effective in increasing well-being as it builds psychological, social, and spiritual resources. (Emmons & McCullough, 2003).

Building supportive interrelationships is clearly an important function of schools today. Moreover, encouraging people to focus on the benefits they have received from others leads them to feel loved and cared for by others. Therefore, gratitude appears to build friendships and other social bonds. These are social resources because, in times of need, these social bonds are wellsprings to be tapped for the provision of social support. Gratitude, thus, is a form of love, a consequence of an already formed attachment as well as a precipitating condition for the formation of new affectional bonds.

Many schools in the UK have some religious affiliation and ethos, and gratitude is also likely to build and strengthen a sense of spirituality, given the strong historical association between gratitude and religious belief. Those who regularly attend religious services and engage in religious activities such as prayer and reading religious material are more likely to be grateful. Grateful people are more likely to acknowledge a belief in the interconnectedness of all life and a commitment and responsibility to others. Gratitude does not require religious faith, but faith enhances the ability to be grateful.

Finally, to the extent that gratitude, like other positive emotions, broadens the scope of cognition, and enables flexible and creative thinking, it also facilitates coping with stress and adversity. According to the broaden-and-build model, gratitude not only makes people feel good in the present, but it also increases the likelihood that people will function optimally and feel good in the future (Emmons & McCullough 2003).

Gratitude Interventions and Psychological and Physical Well-Being

There are compelling reasons why teachers in the UK should take gratitude exercises very seriously. Children who practise grateful thinking have more positive attitudes toward school and their families. In an experimental comparison, those who kept gratitude journals on a weekly basis exercised more regularly, reported fewer physical symptoms, felt better about their lives as a whole, and were more optimistic about the upcoming week compared to those who recorded hassles or neutral life events (Emmons & McCullough, 2003).

A related benefit was observed in the realm of personal goal attainment: participants who kept gratitude lists were more likely to have made progress toward important personal goals (academic, interpersonal and health-based) over a two-month period compared to subjects in the other experimental conditions.

A daily gratitude intervention (self-guided exercises) with young adults resulted in higher reported levels of the positive states of alertness, enthusiasm, determination, attentiveness and energy compared to a focus on hassles or a downward social comparison (ways in which participants thought they were better off than others). There was no difference in levels of unpleasant emotions reported in the three groups.

Participants in the daily gratitude condition were more likely to report having helped someone with a personal problem or having offered emotional support to another.

In a sample of adults with neuromuscular disease, a 21-day gratitude intervention resulted in greater amounts of high energy positive moods, a greater sense of feeling connected to others, more optimistic ratings of one's life, and better sleep duration and sleep quality, relative to a control group.

Encouraging mindfulness in the present

One attribute of consciousness that has been much-discussed in relation to well-being is 'mindfulness'. It is most commonly defined as **the state of being attentive to and aware of what is taking place in the present.** Many philosophical, spiritual, and psychological traditions emphasize the importance of the quality of consciousness for the maintenance and enhancement of well-being. Despite this, it is easy to overlook the importance of consciousness in human well-beings because almost everyone exercises its primary capacities of attention and awareness. Indeed, the relation between qualities of consciousness and well-being has received little empirical attention. This is unsurprising given that society, it can be argued, persists in devaluing the present moment in favour of perpetual distraction, self-absorption, and addiction to a feeling of progress.

Mindfulness captures a quality of consciousness that is characterized by clarity and vividness of current experience and functioning, and thus stands in contrast to the mindless, less awake states of habitual or automatic functioning that may be chronic for many individuals. Mindfulness may be important in disengaging individuals from automatic thoughts, habits, and unhealthy behaviour patterns, and thus could play a key role in fostering informed and self-endorsed behavioural regulation, which has long been associated with well-being enhancement. Further, by adding clarity and vividness to experience, mindfulness may also contribute to well-being and happiness in a direct way

Mindfulness is inherently a state of consciousness. Although awareness and attention to present events and experiences are given features of the human organism, these qualities can vary considerably, from heightened states of clarity and sensitivity to low levels, as in habitual, automatic, mindless, or blunted thought or action.

Mindfulness can be cultivated by practice. This idea has inspired a wide variety of mindfulness-promoting interventions for both medical and general populations.

Mindfulness in schools may facilitate the valuable creation of an interval of time or a gap wherein the pupil is able to view his or her mental landscape, including behavioural options, rather than simply react to interpersonal events. This may make it an important variable in a world where enhanced awareness and the consideration of behavioural consequences appear sorely needed.

Building hope, optimism and achievement in schools and families

Children need to be encouraged to believe that by taking action and working harder, they will get results, even if improvements are modest to begin with. When we succeed, we can generate a step change, however small, in our level of attainment; our self–esteem improves and our self-belief, about our own behaviour and courage, is enhanced. Motivation levels and self-efficacy increase and this leads to more hard work and the fostering of greater coping skills, an up-ward spiral towards higher attainment at school. We might lose our footing momentarily en route when we experience minor setbacks, but our resilience and self -efficacy can be improved through these initial efforts to imagine the process and the beneficial outcomes that will accompany it. This will only work if we go forward on the basis of achieving a personal best on a personal baseline, and not continually comparing and contrasting childrens' scores internally, or worse, setting up a system of streaming, where children are allocated teaching groups for all subjects on the basis of their current performance.

Often visualizing success can have a positive effect on our levels of optimism. The same neurons are at work when we use our mind as a simulator and when we live out these visualizations. The act of visualizing enhances the chances for success and we need to make this visualization as real and vivid, tangible, real (and therefore realizable) as possible. We need to evoke a powerful force, using all the senses, and feeling, seeing, hearing our experiences, making each as real as possible, almost fooling our mind into believing the simulator as matching reality as we possibly can. We can feel the passion, anticipate anxiety, evoke emotions. Great speech writers do this. Visualization helps deal with the problem of nerves and the way nervousness hinders performance. Visualizing brings the necessary calm to perform well at whatever task we are called upon to deliver.

In the professional world of aviation, pilots would never be a success without spending hours on their flight simulator. We also have a perfect simulator in our mind's eye, our imagination. By preparing well, by demonstrating a willingness to work hard at it, we can all achieve more. A great role model here, in the world of sport, is former England Rugby Union international Jonny Wilkinson. Through endless hours of practice and utilizing the power of visualization, blurring the distinction between the real activity and the imaginary, using vivid, inner imaginations, Jonny was able to place himself, psychologically as well as physically, in a position to drop the goal that won England the ultimate symbol of success, the Rugby World Cup, in 2003.
Events lead to thoughts which, in part, drive our emotions. The key is to restore rationality in our thinking to bring about healthier and happier emotions. This is why cognitive behavioural therapy

is as helpful for many as medication as an intervention, an acquired skill that we can learn on our own and teach to others.

We interpret, as optimists, negative emotions in a different way. When negative and painful emotions come our way as a natural part of life, we do not see them as permanent and pervasive, we say that these things will pass and these do not become self-fulfilling prophecies. We interpret positive emotions as part of a spiral upwards, we imagine success: it transforms the way the world is, it chips away at the limiting thoughts to reveal the capacity for growth, joy and happiness.

Objective circumstances matter, but our interpretations are far more important. This is why people who are wealthy can be unhappy yet people who do not thrive materially can experience joy. The question is, where do we focus? Do we see setbacks as an opportunity to develop further, a stumbling block, or a stepping stone? Do we focus on the things that are working or do we focus on the things that are not working? We can look at the same event and derive fundamentally different interpretations.

When we focus on the positive, the positive is accentuated. When we appreciate goodness, goodness appreciates more. Faultfinding is sometimes cathartic but unwarranted faultfinding leads to major consequences. If the only things we find are negative, we will develop a sense of what Seligman calls a 'learned helplessness'. We need to respect reality and establish a healthy balance. This means not to ignore pain, but to take a step back.

We need to develop in our children the beauty of benefit finding, not an unhealthy detachment from reality, but to find the miraculous in the common e.g. the sense of awe that comes from the beauty of the outside environment and nature. Children will benefit from taking the time to appreciate the good things in life, to look at them with fresh eyes, to see the benefits of appreciation. We see beyond the faults of life and form the habit of expressing gratitude.

Chipping away at negativity helps make life extraordinary in terms of life satisfaction.
We thus co-create our reality. We create a win-win situation when we express gratitude to others, contributing to others' well-being and also benefitting ourselves in the process. We feel better, generate a real spike in our emotional life, which can be supported by writing gratitude letters and journals to habitualise the feeling of well-being. We enjoy the experience, creating an upwards spiral that benefits the giver and receiver.

It seems to me that many of the efforts that are designed to promote 'self help' concentrate in an unbalanced way on correcting personality weaknesses and areas of development. The strength of the positive psychological approach seems to be that it is less concerned with correcting potential weaknesses but building and broadening our strengths . We spend so much time, energy and money in pursuit of the pleasurable life that we quickly become habituated to it. The pleasant life has limits. Before too long, we run out of opportunities because the list is finite. Similarly, this is the greatest danger for those of us bringing up our own children who seem to have an almost insatiable thirst for more and more material gadgets and toys, a need fed by an voracious advertising machine. We do not want our children to miss out, yet we fail to see the dangers in acceding to their every request even without building in some future orientation or reward system.

Talking straight, I have drawn the conclusion that the greatest sense of well-being is when we recognize that our happiest moments come through our experience of the good life, where we produce abundant authentic happiness by playing to our signature strengths. We need first of all to recognize what those strengths might be, and so it would be a good idea to check out the inventory (free of charge) on the VIA Institute of Character website at authentic happiness.com.

My current inventory reads like this:

Your Top Strength

Leadership
You excel at the tasks of leadership: encouraging a group to get things done and preserving harmony within the group by making everyone feel included. You do a good job organizing activities and seeing that they happen.

Your Second Strength

Gratitude
You are aware of the good things that happen to you, and you never take them for granted. Your friends and family members know that you are a grateful person because you always take the time to express your thanks.

Your Third Strength

Forgiveness and mercy
You forgive those who have done you wrong. You always give people a second chance. Your guiding principle is mercy and not revenge.

I would say that this is a pretty positive and accurate depiction of my signature strengths and that I can see how expressing them could be the source of my gratifications – attaining 'the full life' - in my professional career and at home. These have to be located, too, in something beyond the good life.

Seligman does not attempt to offer a complete epistemology or full theory of meaning. We do, moreover, need to raise the bar in our aspirations for happiness beyond the next box of chocolate or glass of champagne and further our work to find full gratification through expressing our signature strengths. I have found this meaning through a lively and active Christian faith that has been nurtured from those early East End days.

Moving from theory to practice

Seligman has designed and tested interventions to nurture each of the three routes to happiness (pleasure, gratification and meaning). These research designs are exactly parallel to the random-assignment, placebo-controlled experiments that are the bulwark of the medication and psychotherapy outcome literature, except that the intervention is targeted to increase happiness rather just to decrease suffering. One reason for optimism that the field of Positive Psychology may make substantial gains in the next several years is that it starts from a firm empirical base: it draws on the proven psychological methodologies.

1. Positive emotions are increased and the pleasant life is promoted by exercises that increase gratitude, that increase savouring, that build optimism and that challenge discouraging beliefs about the past. The 'good things in life' exercise provides an example of an efficacious intervention. Designed to increase positive emotion about the past, this exercise requires individuals to record, every day for a week, three good things that happened to them each day and why those good things occurred. After completing this exercise, individuals were happier and less depressed at the three-month follow-up (Seligman & Steen 2005).

2. Interventions that increase the good life identify participants' signature strengths and use them more often and in creative new ways.

3. Meaningful life interventions aim toward participants' identifying and connecting with something larger than themselves by using their signature strengths

Early results demonstrate that it is possible to boost individuals' levels of happiness, and these effects do not fade immediately after the intervention (as is the case with the placebo).

Conclusions

From this theoretical base, teachers can offer practical suggestions to achieve the following as learning objectives:

a. Enjoy and celebrate the good things in the present with an active appreciation of what one has. This can be done very effectively in tutor time, school assemblies and other corporate school events.
b. Harnessing strengths from day to day, broadening and building positive emotions because positive emotions appear to *broaden* people's momentary thought-action repertoires and *build* their enduring personal resources. Through experiences of positive emotions people *transform* themselves, becoming more creative, knowledgeable, resilient, socially integrated, and healthy individuals .
This can be dome by adopting a character building word of the week and encouraging activities to support the practice of the desirable trait.
c. To have positive reminiscences and reconciliation with the past. This can be corporately through recognizing unique school traditions and recounting of the founder's mission, vision and values.
d. Dealing effectively with negative events through firm but fair behavioural management policies
e. Investing in close and social connections e.g. through planned team, orchestra and house activities and organized Parents' Association events.
f. Working towards goals with strategic intents that are aligned with values and are intrinsically motivating. This could be for a teaching group to agree specific objectives for the year or via target setting sessions and academic tutorials with parents.

Bearing in mind Kurt Lewin's maxim (1951: 169) that there is nothing so practical as a good theory, some workable suggestions to help support teachers are offered in the next chapter.

Chapter 5: Ten practical suggestions for school settings.

> *'Good, the more communicated, more abundant grows'.*
> John Milton, *Paradise Lost*, Book V

There are some key applications that can be made by teachers in order to put into practice some of the theoretical propositions made by Seligman and his colleagues. The truth is that the pursuit of happiness is not to be found in quite easy fixes or a lifeless list of attributes. It involves hard work. It involves action on the part of those who regard themselves as possessing a degree of practical idealism, a motivation that brought many teachers into the profession in the first place.

It is a central contention here that school teachers need to cultivate an appreciative perspective. They need to recognise that negative events are more potent than positive events and that particularly negative feedback after tasks is more potent than positive feedback. When combining negative and positive feedback, the negative tends to come out stronger.

In recent UK research (Mayall, 2007) has emphasized young adolescents' desire for positive pupil-teacher relationships. As Rudduck and Flutter (2004) have argued, what was striking about teachers identified by young people as 'good' was that 'the qualities that mattered to pupils tended to be as much about how they were *treated* as how they were taught' The implications for teachers are clearly demonstrated by McLaughlin and Clarke (2010) when they stress the importance of positive teacher pupil relationships. This is a key insight offered here, that this relationship is fundamental to the establishment of schools as a place of psychological safety. Morris (2009) asserts that children adopt teachers as role models without first asking permission, and the way that relationships are conducted with those taught are being closely observed whether we like it or not. This assertion is not new: individuals remember their most effective teachers partly because they give us clues about how life ought to be lived that went beyond the teaching of discrete subject material.

An accusation could be leveled that this emphasis on the psycho-social needs of pupils as a counter balance to the purely academic dimension is a trend that we have seen before e.g. through the child-centric vestiges of the Plowden Report (1967). That report was widely known for its praising of child-centred approaches to education, stressing that 'at the heart of the educational process lies the child'. The new educational context, moreover, demands differing priorities and approaches that herald a whole system change.

This approach is not to be confused with some of the more cult-like adherents of the self-help movement. Some sell groundless, New Age, fantastical ideas that are both false and ultimately detrimental to the people who buy into them. We are not talking here about delusional thinking, from extreme Pollyanna-like optimism, to the idea that if you wish for something hard enough, it will magically 'manifest' itself in your life. My suggestions here comprise simple interventions and are offered in the light of over thirty years continuous service in schools. This experience has generated an understanding of the micro issues of individual child psychology, (refined through the crucible of observation and activity in classrooms around the world) and the macro experience of living through the consequences of the past three decades of turbulent educational history in the UK.

1. Firstly, as educationalists we need to develop an **appreciative approach** to our enquiries. A key research methodology at the National College for School Leadership for Schools and Children's Services where I am a Research Associate, is an approach known as appreciative enquiry. It is an obvious approach to researching and delivering well-being in schools with its emphasis on appreciating the best elements of school-based activity. It is appropriate at this stage to examine the provenance of this approach for those unfamiliar with the concept.

In the 1980s, Dr David Cooperrider, Suresh Srivasta and colleagues at Case Western Reserve University, Cleveland, US began challenging the models of change management and problem-solving that were in use at the time. They challenged the conventional assumptions which suggest that individuals and groups operate in a stable and lasting environment. Instead, they proposed that the environment is continually changing and that what individuals and groups deem to be reality is merely a product of the moment, giving rise to infinite possibilities for reconstruction moment by moment. Set in this context, it may be argued that traditional approaches, when applied to the evaluation of learning and development, encourage backward reflection in isolation from forward thinking. Cooperrider (1987) created a theory and approach to living with change called Appreciative Enquiry, proposing a particular set of assumptions:

Six elements of Appreciative Enquiry

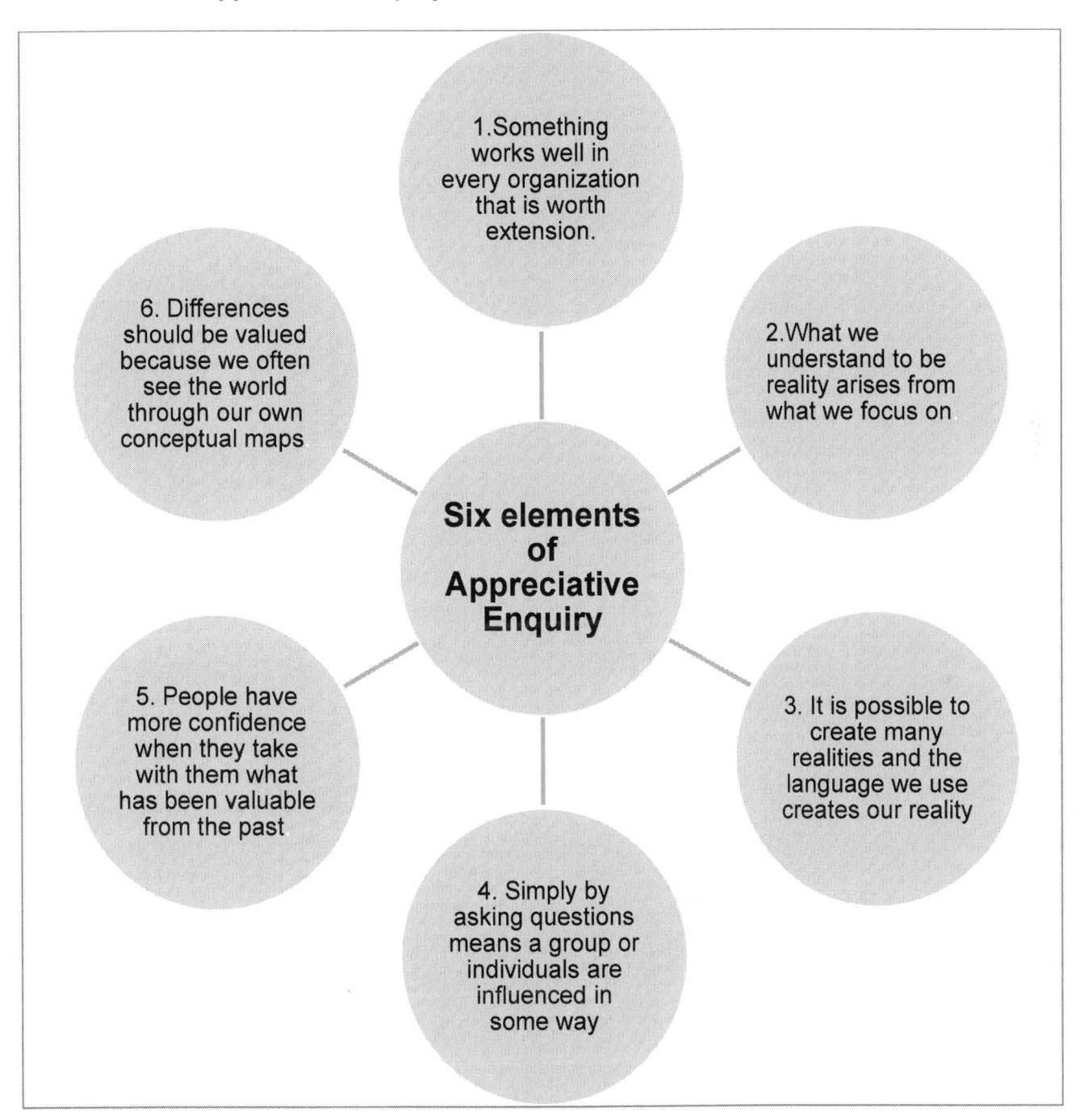

- 1. Something works well in every organization that is worth extension.
- 2. What we understand to be reality arises from what we focus on.
- 3. It is possible to create many realities and the language we use creates our reality
- 4. Simply by asking questions means a group or individuals are influenced in some way
- 5. People have more confidence when they take with them what has been valuable from the past
- 6. Differences should be valued because we often see the world through our own conceptual maps

Adapted by Lee (2012)

Cooperrider and Srivasta suggested that organizations are in a continual state of emergence. The traditional organizational development processes focused attention on defining a problem, sought to fix it, then tried to measure or assess whether the solution had actually worked. Appreciative Enquiry, however, seeks to encourage people to search for what already works well, and to amplify this. This thinking challenges conventional approaches to organizational development, perhaps suggesting they offer little of value in contemporary organizations, and that interventions such as Strengths, Weaknesses, Opportunities, Threats benchmarking, gap analysis and performance indicators, should be replaced. This would allow leaders to gain new insights and perspectives on what are arguably more challenging approaches to coping with change.

Following on from this philosophical position, I adopted an Appreciative Enquiry approach in the data collection for this book. This included the survey design as well as a semi-structured interview schedule when interviewing school leaders in the case study school. Here a 'Four Delta approach' was adopted as an organizing principle.

Discover
- Look at what is working best: appreciate and know the best of our life together so far. Know what we have to build on.

Dream
- Consider what might be, create a future memory, picture the results.

Design
- What does the ideal look like? People create shared images, understand where they fit, are connected, are valued. They create synergy to realise the dream / strategy.

Deliver
- Self-enpowerment, learning, adjustment or improvisation, sustainability and increased energy help deliver the dream.

The Four Delta Principle (adapted by Lee 2012)

In schools and families, we have to continue to focus on the positive. Schools are unique in that they provide a common-room for teaching staff to associate in the course of the working day. Because of the negativity bias, a school culture can easily become one where teachers corporately whine about the difficulty of the task, the unreasonableness of the children in their charge, the general poverty of their lot.

We all know of colleagues who use our energy by their constant gripes. When the common room is predominantly negative, this impacts on the effectiveness of the school, creating an unhelpful ethos. We know that teaching is a very demanding job, often conducted in challenging circumstances with challenging personnel. However, the negative attitude should never be tolerated because it ultimately impacts on the children. Who can blame their pupils being unhappy if their role models and mentors demonstrate the potency of negativity so effectively? Teachers must accentuate the positive – complain less, look for and appreciate the goodness in situations, praise others for their strength, and present alternatives where there are obstacles.

The work of school leaders is so important in this regard. They set the tone for the organization in their oral and written communications, but so much more so in their behaviour, their demeanour, their body language. Their role-modeling of a better way is absolutely crucial for happier schools, for they can demonstrate effectively the virtue of becoming benefit finders who seek and create good in the world.

The truth is that the well-being of pupils in schools is utterly dependent on the re-vivification of the teachers in schools. Critics of a positive psychological approach in the world of work are somehow appalled at the idea of leaders and managers showing an interest in having happy employees - heaven forbid!

Pupil well-being has its genesis in teacher well-being. Teachers, as well as everyone else, can learn that added wealth brings no further life satisfaction and that the myth of happiness is related directly to youthfulness: life satisfaction goes up with age. The truth is that climate, race and gender – none of them much matters for happiness. Marriage, sociability and religious belief, moreover, are robustly related to happiness (Seligman 2003). In addition, Valliant's respected longitudinal research with Harvard graduates identifies seven major factors that predict healthy ageing:

a. Employing mature adaptations (unconscious responses to pain, conflict and uncertainty): these thoughts can either shape or distort an individual's reality
b. a good education
c. stable marriage
d. not smoking
e. not abusing alcohol
f. some exercise
g. maintaining a healthy weight

Depression turns out to be a major negative factor on physical health. Alcoholism is a main driver of pathology, unsurprisingly. Valliant also draws attention to the power of relationships as a social aptitude that leads to successful ageing. When asked about the key learnings of the Grant study in the March 2008 newsletter, Valliant responded that 'the only thing that really matters in life is your relationships to other people'. This underscores again the importance of the quality of interpersonal relationships in school settings in all their forms.

It is progress when an employer makes it a point to ensure that his/ her employees are happy, their well-being coinciding with his / her effort to maximize efficiency, not conflict with it. The amoral, dictator-style Head would now actually have an incentive to treat his staff well. The slave driver whipping the backs of the teachers would be run out of business by the savvy principal next door, whose workforce is happy and eager to do excellent work.

I think most teachers would rather have a Head who had a vested interest in ensuring their happiness and well-being, than one who knew that the more he could abuse them, the better off he and the bottom line would be. Quite simply, I'd rather my Head benefit from my happiness than my misery.

Positive Psychology therefore sides with the teachers, although it would be more accurate to say that Positive Psychology sides with both the teacher and management. This incorporates a sense of self-acceptance, so that successful teachers can see and accept their strengths and weaknesses. They enjoy a clear sense of purpose in their professional life, reflecting the strategic leadership present in the school, in that they enjoy professional, realisable goals and objectives that give meaning and direction to their daily work.

Attempting to nurture happiness in the work place is not a quick fix. It requires protracted efforts in order to produce results. In the current economic climate, for example, there are plenty of instances of schools that have been grossly mismanaged, engaged in quick, mindless and careless initiatives, and then have brought in some life coach, 'uber-consultant' or 'super-head' in order to make sure there was a positive working environment. This is akin to 'putting icing on mud.'

The best leaders in schools, as in all organizations, appreciate goodness. In other words they recognize the best in people and as they do so, goodness appreciates from within the organization. They battle against the waves of bad news that flood through the media that, unchallenged, feed an organizational culture of doom and despondency. They use other sources of information such as Gimundo and the Good News network that actively seek to spread the benefit of good occurrences in the world. They provide a wonderful balance for children who are bombarded with the latest sensationalist exclusive from the tabloids.

Teachers in schools that are well led have a sense of personal growth. They feel that their personal and unique talents and potential are being realized over time. In successful schools, people have positive professional relations with others and also enjoy close valued connections with significant others in their personal lives. The best school leaders foster in their teachers a sense of professional mastery in that they enable them to thrive in managing the demands of everyday life. The best teachers also demonstrate a developed sense of autonomy, displaying the strength to follow personal convictions even if they go against conventional practices.

The best leaders create a spiral of growth that is grounded in reality. They have learned the truth that there is always something to appreciate in schools if you look hard enough. Furthermore, they understand that if good is not appreciated, it depreciates. They realize that they must not wait for something external and extraordinary to happen before they learn to appreciate the ordinary. In schools it is a matter of practice, of encouraging the art of appreciation over and over again, till it becomes second nature.

Appreciating the beauties of the natural world is often a good starting point. In the words of Helen Keller:

> *'I wondered how it was possible to walk for an hour through the woods and see nothing of note. I who cannot see find hundreds of things: the delicate symmetry of a leaf, the smooth skin of a silver birch, the rough, shaggy bark of a pine. I who am blind can give one hint to those who see: use your eyes as if tomorrow you will have been stricken blind. Hear the music of voices, the songs of a bird, the mighty strains of an orchestra as if you would be stricken deaf tomorrow. Touch each object as if tomorrow your tactile sense would fail. Smell the perfume of flowers, taste with relish each morsel, as if tomorrow you could never taste or smell again. Make the most of every sense. Glory in all the facets and pleasures and beauty which the world reveals to you.'*

Finding pleasure in the natural world is a key to well-being in austerity Britain

In practical terms, there are a number of activities that the pupils can do to re-iterate a sense of appreciation.

- They need to be given time to reflect, either in tutor time or together in assemblies.

- Teachers know best. Put away the practice SATS papers for a moment. Use the outdoors as far as possible to encourage a sense of awe and wonder, particularly in Key Stage 1 and the earlier part of Key Stage 2. Much is being made of the Forest School movement as part of Finland's educational success and this can be emulated as long as the children have appropriate clothing to enjoy the outdoors, given the vagaries of the weather.

- Pupils can be encouraged to keep gratitude diaries – three things they are grateful for in any given week. This has proven psychological benefits if adopted as a regular practice. Not only are there benefits to health, but encouraging pupils to open up by writing about emotional topics has been found to reduce anxiety and depression and improve grades in school.

- They can be encouraged to write letters, phone, visit people in person to express their gratitude – to grandparents, members of the wider family, sports coaches, music teachers, subject specialists, indeed anyone who has directly helped them in some way. Research suggests that this will lead to the largest boost in well-being if habitualised regularly (weekly, bi-weekly or monthly)

- Appreciative writing helps even if the letter of appreciation is not sent.

- On a different level, the act of rationalizing our emotional concerns by writing about them has shown to yield benefits. This includes keeping a daily journal. Pennebaker, (1997) demonstrated that writing honestly about emotional challenges in his student group led to reduced anxiety, a 50% drop in visits to the doctor, improvements in immune system and overall health, and a increase in general emotional well-being.

Gratefulness then becomes an authentic measure of well-being. We become stiffened to whatever we take for granted and deadened to the beauties of life if we are numbed and noncommittal in our outlook. We need to encourage our pupils to strive to consistently check that they not taking any of the wonderful things in their life for granted because they have 'become used to them'.

2. The **second** way we can encourage pupils to develop a better sense of well-being is by creating more opportunities for them to experience a sense of flow. I would argue that this is not merely the province of the aesthetic subjects but that flow should be achieved in all areas of the curriculum.

Across the cultural divide there are some psychological components that appear ubiquitous. There are times in life when time seems to stop. We are doing exactly what we want to be doing and there is a real sense that we do not want this experience to end. We don't tend to feel much at the time in terms of positive emotion although this might be considered retrospectively. We find flow when a task is challenging and requires skill but we are up to it. We concentrate so fully on the task in hand that we are no longer absorbed by our self and whatever is troubling us. There are clear goals for us to achieve and we get immediate feedback on how well we are doing. We are deeply, effortlessly involved in what we are doing and we experience a sense of control.

The research seems to suggest that the optimal experience is enjoyed readily by some but not at all by others. Low flow teenagers are often those who hang around shopping malls a lot and watch a great deal of television. High flow teenagers have hobbies, engage in sport and spend quite a time on homework.

While all this engagement is perceived as not as much fun, it certainly pays off in terms of access to higher education, deeper social ties, and success in later life. This perception that the gratifications are not always fun is problematic in that we often chose pleasure over gratification – many times we would rather watch tv than read a good book. We tend to habitually choose the pleasures over gratification. We tend to take the short cuts to happiness through easy-win, pleasure-seeking than through the higher goals of gratification or finding meaning. This can set us up for disappointment or even depression. Our strengths may atrophy if they do not find expression over a period of time.

Flow (an optimal, psychological experience) is promoted by

- A challenging activity where we are neither overwhelmed nor underwhelmed. It is utterly vital that we start from where the pupils are in their understanding. We constantly check to see what they already know, understand and can do. If we underpitch, they will be bored; over pitch it then they will be lost. The Vygotskian principle of the zone of proximal learning is hugely important to our understanding in this regard.

- If our classroom activities are stimulating, there arises a merging of action and awareness. We therefore aim at nurturing full attention to the task in hand - we become one with what we are doing in a deep, effortless involvement.

- To achieve the flow state, we need to establish clear goals and give immediate feedback where possible.

- In these best lessons, the sense of self vanishes and we are not bound by the clock.

- We can identify our pupils' signature strengths through the use of simple self-reported inventories – see www.authentichappiness.com for exemplifications.

- We then encourage pupils to use their signature strengths as far as possible every day. Flow occurs when the challenges mesh well with   our abilities. We should reflect on how to re-craft our work to use our strengths more and produce more flow.

We can encourage greater well-being by creating more opportunities for flow

3.The **third** practical way to improve pupil well-being is a simple intervention designed to increase optimism and hope particularly by improving our self-explanatory style or self-talk by disputing pessimistic thoughts. We all are subject to judgemental, interior thoughts, the difference being that our inner judges always find us guilty to a greater or lesser extent! To counter this inner negativity, a simple self-disputation can be most effective. This can be best described diagrammatically.

The background to this intervention is a US model called the Penn Resiliency programme (PRP). It is clearly a cognitive behavioural intervention that teaches pupils to change their beliefs gradually that are shaping mal-adaptively their emotions.

> 'It encourages them to keep a sense of perspective; to think outside of the box and more flexibly about the multiple and varied causes of problems (self-disputing and to restrict the tendency to catastrophise that fuels negative thoughts. All of this aims to develop a young person's emotional and social competence' (Young 2009).

Young also cites the fact that eleven evaluations of the PRP show it can cut teenage depression by up to half and bad behaviour by a third.

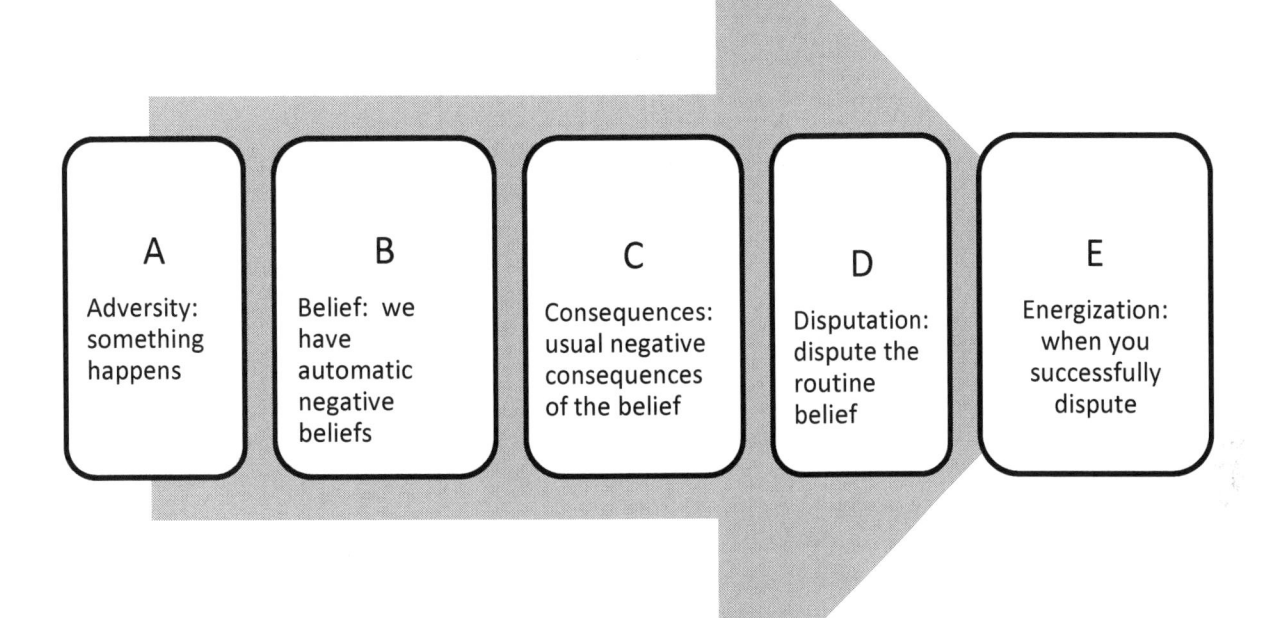

A	B	C	D	E
Adversity: something happens	Belief: we have automatic negative beliefs	Consequences: usual negative consequences of the belief	Disputation: dispute the routine belief	Energization: when you successfully dispute

Staff can thus encourage pupils to learn to argue with incorrect self- beliefs – the most convincing way of disputing a negative belief is to show it is factually incorrect. Then they should be encouraged to look for alternative explanations – scan for all possible contributing causes and finally de-catastrophize – by asking, 'how likely is the worse-case scenario?' Additionally, pupils can be encouraged to avoid the three m's – Magnifying, Minimizing and Making up e.g.

1. Magnifying (exaggerating)
    a. Permanent and Pervasive (over-generalizing)
    b. All-or-nothing thinking

2. Minimizing (underplaying)
    a. Tunnel vision – dispute the rationality, let's be real.
    b. Dismissal of positive or negative

3. Making up (fabricating)
    a. Personalization or blame
    b. Emotional reasoning

Resilience is the process of adapting well in the face of adversity, tragedy, or high levels of stress. It has been used to mean the processes by which children, youth, and adults *withstand* those sources of challenge and also the patterns of *bouncing back* or *recovering* from such conditions. Over the past few decades the psychological sciences have seen a tremendous growth in the number of research studies focusing on resilience. During this time we have learned a great deal about the personal, social, and societal factors that help individuals succeed despite being exposed to adversity. This information has been used to guide new approaches to interventions with children and adolescents who have developed, or are at risk of developing, serious emotional disorders.

Seligman (2002) has proposed that common tactics used by experienced and competent professionals, such as building rapport, trust, opening up, and naming the problem, all serve to produce positive therapeutic outcomes. He also recommends another class of techniques, 'deep strategies,' that are commonly used by effective professionals and include such things as instilling hope and building buffering strengths. The buffering strengths, such things as optimism, interpersonal skills, future-mindedness, and finding a purpose, all reflect a resilience, or strengths-based approach to treatment.

The traits of resilience can be cultivated. Pupils can be encouraged to be reflective (making sense of their own thoughts, feelings and emotions), to increase a growing awareness of agency (the conviction that we can intervene effectively in their life) and nurture a better degree of relatedness, a sense of engagement and interaction with others. Resilient children display an optimistic bias, a drive for mastery, which focuses on the upside of life. Teachers can promote a greater sense of resilience by helping pupils to identify some common cognitive distortions. They sometimes need to challenge their own explanatory style – the self-talk that we are all engaged in to explain our experiences in life; these include:

- **All or nothing:** everything either a success of failure. We restore rationality by disputing this.
- **Blame:** thinking others are totally responsible for your actions.
- **Catastrophising:** increasing your anxiety by expecting the worst outcome, manufacturing fear through using 'what if' statements.
- **Over generalisation**: assuming too much from too little.
- **Mental filtering**: selecting a small detail that confirms an inadequacy.
- **Mind reading**: believing you know what others are thinking.
- **Fortune telling:** claiming to know what would happen if things were different.
- **Magnification**: overestimating the significance of an event.
- **Emotional reasoning:** using only what you initially feel to determine the truth of a situation.
- **Labelling:** making global statements about yourself.
- **Personalisation:** thinking you are totally responsible for another's actions.

In addition, teachers can take a biographical approach by studying resilience through the lives of the people who have faced significant points of adversity in their lives and made it through to the other side. We need to tell the children the constructive narrative of the ordinary person who turns the dream of making the most of his / her abilities himself into a meaningful reality.

Most importantly in my view, we should take heed of resilience studies that show that one good relationship that can act as a catalyst and an opening to a richer life. This is the true vocation of the teaching profession, to make a difference and to be available to the needy minority that have no helpful others around.

Fourthly, in terms of feedback that teachers provide, they can do much to help pupils by avoiding harmful praise (Dweck, 2005). Dweck has discovered that around 40% of pupils have a fixed mind set – they believe they are intelligent or stupid and that this is fixed. Hindered by these closed minds, bright students whose marks dipped thought that they were dumb after all whereas pupils who were praised for their efforts saw the setback as a signal for more effort.

This means that teachers should be emphasizing the effort that pupils have put in as well as their creativity in problem solving, as opposed to merely praising natural intelligence:

> *'Emphasizing effort gives a child a variable that they can control. They come to see themselves as in control of their success. Emphasizing natural intelligence takes it out of the child's control, and it provides no good recipe for responding to a failure'*

and

> *'When you praise kids' intelligence and then they fail, they think they're not smart anymore, and they lose interest in their work. In contrast, kids praised for effort show no impairment and often are energized in the face of difficulty.'*

Pupils need to learn the important life lesson that it is acceptable to fail. It's ok to fail because no one is perfect. As teachers we don't want to deprive our children of living a full and enjoyable life because they experience fear about their own capabilities. Persistence or effort is often the hidden factor behind those considered gifted.

Many creative geniuses were not born that way. They were often fairly ordinary people who became **extraordinarily motivated**. These people did not just have a desire to achieve but also a love of learning, a love of challenge and the ability to thrive on obstacles to progress. These attributes of persistence, rigour and passion are indeed, the greatest gifts we can give our pupils.

We need to encourage pupils to risk doing new things as opportunities arise and if they do fail, to take time to learn from their failures. Rather than trying to be perfect, pupils are sometimes very hesitant to display any emotion because they feel that they are revealed to be weak. They need to be given permission to be human and tell themselves that it is acceptable to feel emotions, accept them, and work through them.

When we praise children regardless of whether they have earned it or not, we create a number of problems for ourselves. A pupil may have trouble later in understanding where he or she has succeeded when praise is given sincerely. Additionally, children might remain passive because they have learned that praise is going to come their way whatever actions they take. We naturally want the children to feel positively about themselves all the time as they sometimes express disappointment in schools that they have not been praised or that they have not been praised enough. We have to guard against the dangers of empty praise and seek to reward effort and ingenuity.

Fifthly, teachers would do well to create a positive atmosphere in classrooms by creating an aspirational motto that is shared at the beginning of each lesson that re-iterates an ethos of expectation, optimism and hope. Sir Michael Wilshaw, Chief Inspector of Schools, has demonstrated the potency of this methodology at Mossbourne Community Academy in Hackney where pupils recite at the start of each lesson:

> 'I aspire to maintaining inquiring mind, a calm disposition and an
> attentive ear so that in this class and in all classes I can fulfill my
> true potential'

Sixthly, it would be wrong to underplay the importance of regular exercise as a methodology to improve pupil well-being. Obesity increases the risk for type 2 diabetes, cardiovascular disease, and some cancers. A typical fast-food meal (double cheeseburger soft drink, fries, and a dessert) can contain, at 2,200 kilocalories, enough energy to power a 120-pound person through an entire marathon. With this type of regular diet, children and teenagers are contracting adult-onset diabetes at a rapidly increasing pace. Among healthy people, exercise can raise levels of HDL, or good cholesterol, improve clotting factors, lower blood pressure, and decrease inflammation. All of these factors reduce
the risk of cardiovascular disease.

The single thing that comes close to a magic bullet, in terms of its strong and universal benefits, is exercise. Exercise can change virtually every tissue in the body, but because it works by many different pathways - metabolic, hormonal, neurological, and mechanical - understanding why and how it works, in an integrated way, is not easy. The most fundamental development in behavioural medicine is the recognition that we can no longer think about health as being solely a characteristic of the body or the mind because body and mind are interconnected.

Exercise works on anxiety, on panic disorder, and on stress in general, which has a lot to do with depression. And it generates the release of neurotransmitters, norepinephrine, serotonin, and dopamine, that are very similar to our most important psychiatric medicines. Not exercising can be construed in the same way as agreeing to take a daily depressant!

It would be wrong to underplay the importance of regular exercise as a methodology to improve pupil well-being.

Teachers and families can help children by:

A Providing **knowledge** for them to learn more about what exercise can do for them.
B Becoming **aspirational**: suggesting a realistic goal to work towards.
C Encouraging pupils to **monitor progress**: by using a pedometer, or perhaps keep a log of what they do. These tools will let pupils track their progress.
D **Developing Patience**: changes in the body occur slowly. People who are
trying to lose weight in particular need to give it time.
E **Social support:** encouraging classmates to share their efforts will improve consistency.
F Suggest **variety**: by encouraging pupils to try out new activities. Weight-train, row, swim, or roller-skate. Cross-training is good for physical and mental well-being. A disco dancing class might be a novel introduction to the benefits of regular exercise.
G **Strategy**: increase your activity by taking the stairs instead of an escalator or lift, or getting off one stop early when riding public transportation.
H **Options**: have indoor and outdoor options so that you can't make excuses whenever the weather is bad. Try a new class, join a gym, or purchase home exercise equipment.

Seventhly, there are proven benefits demonstrated through the regular practice of mindfulness meditation: the possibility for mood change, an increase in pre-frontal cortex activation and an improvement in the immune response. Such inner activity enhances self-esteem, induces calm and improves thinking. Meditation is a conscious effort to focus attention in a non-critical, non-analytical way. Regular practice can lead to a reduction in fearful, anxious thinking, promoting a sense of calm.

It is so important to find something to savour in our everyday experience of school. This teaches such an important life lesson. There are moments in the school day where we can switch off the reminders of other things that will be done during the day or wondering what comes next, or considering how things can be improved. This can occur through encouraging children to focus on certain elements and blocking out others, listening to music whilst closing one's eyes, concentrating on the pleasing aroma of a scented candle. This may be seen by some as a luxury that we can ill afford, but we do have time in schools – the question is how we are going to allocate this time and how to make it a priority in the business of the working week. We need to find techniques to increase a sense of savouring in the lives of our pupils, basking in earned praise and congratulation, thanksgiving as we express gratitude for the good things in our lives, marvelling as we lose a sense of self in the wonder of the moment and even the opportunity to luxuriate as we indulge in our senses.

As an inspector of schools, I am mandated to evaluate the sense of social, moral, spiritual and cultural elements in a school. What better methodologies exist to develop these essential non-academic elements of school life?

Cultivating mindfulness can lead to the discovery of deep realms of relaxation, calmness, and insight within yourself. The benefits include a decrease in anxiety. Mindfulness means seeing things as they are, without trying to change them. It is well within the bounds of possibility for each lesson to begin with a simple breathing exercise. If I had to limit my advice on healthier living to just one tip, it would be simply to learn how to breathe correctly: make our breathing deeper, quieter, slower, and more regular. In doing so we are making our body function better, quieting our mind and serving to harmonize our nervous system.

There are also benefits associated in raising awareness by promoting appropriate levels of sleep. Effects of sleep deprivation on health and well-being have been documented by research. Cognitive skills and physical performance are impaired by sleep deprivation, but mood is affected even more. People who get less than a full night's sleep are prone to feel less happy, more stressed, more physically frail and more mentally and physically exhausted as a result. Sufficient sleep makes us feel better, happier, more vigorous and vital. Mindfulness exercises at bedtime can certainly help achieve better sleep.

Eighthly, a positive environment can be created to encourage well-being, for example surrounding the pupils with inspiring people, pictures, quotes, positive research, reading / watching inspirational media, promotion of peacefulness. This has major implications for the way we arrange and decorate our classrooms and corridors.

Ninthly, time could be spent in tutor time to discuss how we go about making changes in our behaviour. Children have yet to overcome some negative habits and institute some positive ones, like exercise, because they either start out with a plan that is too aggressive or give up when they don't do it. They need to create rituals, make definite commitments and live up to those commitments. When I take action, things happen. If I sit around and plan and plan and plan and plan, nothing happens. Sometimes I need to 'just do it'.

This activity could take the form of a discussion about taking small actions towards a goal and ritualizing these changes. This moves the children away from a message that is solely centred on the need for self-discipline to simple actions that can become habitualised through the creation of daily rituals. It takes 30 days to establish a new ritualized behaviour e.g. an increase in exercise levels, daily breathing exercises, writing a journal. We give our pupils permission to be human, to learn from their mistakes and journalize the unpleasant experiences if they become too painful. We can ritualize deep breathing exercises by executing them throughout the day (i) at mid-morning break, (ii) on the occasions that they are lining up, (iii.) at any lull in the proceedings, waiting for the start of a lesson etc.

This type of simple behavioural change can lead to positive increases in productivity and creativity. The key thought here is the need for action to achieve change in contrast to constant rumination. Change is difficult. When I change a pattern, I work at one thing at a time for 30 days. And then I start to work on the next thing to change.

Physical posture is also important and it would be good to ritualize an alert, upright stance, a firm handshake, a smiling countenance and a good humoured, mannered approach. This will make an enormous difference to the way pupils view the world and have an immediate impact on school culture.

Lastly, useful time can be sent in discussing the part that having self-concordant goals can be of benefit for our well-being and happiness. Life is a journey of compelling milestones: I enjoy the journey by having self-concordant goals and by maintaining the necessary belief, desire, and persistence (especially when faced with inevitable failures and setbacks) required in their pursuit. I fail more, and learn from my failures. When pupils find the things they can do, they get better at everything. **The straightforward approach is that social and emotional competencies do not supersede cognitive abilities so we need to create the schools where they reinforce one another.**

Chapter 6: Positive Psychology- a stumbling block or stepping stone?

The Positive Psychology approach is not without its critics. There are examples of a showdown at the happiness hotel. A *New York Times Magazine* feature even said 'Positive Psychology can seem like a retro endeavor with the appeal of a cure that fits on a recipe card' and refers to the 'sect like feel of Positive Psychology.' Barbara Ehrenreich argues that the 'epidemic of forced cheerfulness' and the 'happiness industry' are partly responsible for 'some big bummers, everything from our slide into war to the economic crisis'.

Ehrenreich is critical of 'bogus' and 'false' and 'unsullied' optimism. Such specific modifiers mean that there must be a 'genuine,' 'real' and 'authentic' optimism — something imperfect but grounded in reality. Realistic optimism is the bedrock of Positive Psychology — the scientific study of well-being. When carefully defined, optimism is about seeing opportunity in challenge, identifying the limitations of bad events and finding hope in the most dire of times.

Ehrenreich's position is to say, 'Well, but it feels nice to be positive. I do all this work on myself and become more positive, and I feel better.' She says, 'You might feel better if you stopped doing all that work on yourself.' This is a burden people take on. Just put that aside. Don't fuss all the time about your mood and your attitude. Try to deal with the world itself.

Her polemic attack on the entire field of Positive Psychology needs to be addressed. Her misunderstanding and/or misrepresentation is almost entirely unjustified and is evidence of a possible popular and equally damaging misconception, that is to say people equating new age superstition with the evidence-based science of Positive Psychology. Positive Psychology is fundamentally different. Associating it with the 'Positive Thinking' movement is like equating Astronomy with Astrology.

It is possible to argue that Ehrenreich did the world a favour by pointing out how Positive Psychology can be misconstrued. A good debate about positive thinking and optimism is not a bad thing at all, more an opportunity to present the research and data that backs up the scientific study behind Positive Psychology, to bring it to mainstream attention.

This section aims to address some possible objections to the foundations of the Positive Psychology movement by a critical readership, adopting a simple question and answer methodology:

Question: Is Positive Psychology an exercise in wishful thinking?

Answer: There seems to be a less than rigorous argument in putting Positive Psychology on level ground with the fringe. It seems to me that it is possible to criticize the relentless and unfounded optimism displayed by the positive thinking adherents whose approach is not backed up by anything more than wishful thinking and a desperate desire to believe in the message of the self-help books. On the other hand, at this point, the body of evidence drawn from research into positivity and happiness, and particularly its potential on UK school children, is too vast, too long-standing, and too persuasive to be dismissed.

The core scientific findings of Positive Psychology are

- an emphasis on taking actions as the cornerstone for change, learning from failure and the role of suffering as elements for growth.
- It encourages realistic ambition, a rejection of perfectionism and an aspiration to adopt moderate and reasonable standards.
- Positive Psychology centres on a balanced interpretation of the negative experience the acceptance of reality as a vital attributes for a fulfilled life.
- Positive Psychology has many facets, but the most radical and essential one, it seems to me, is its grounding in research.

The critical difference between self-help and Positive Psychology is evidence - solid, extensively researched, scientifically grounded principles - not fanciful conjectures made by self-appointed gurus. Positive Psychology needs to be cognizant of its reputation and make it a point to bolster, maintain, and defend itself with vigilance. A tarnished reputation wouldn't just be unfortunate to those working in the field, but could potentially result in untold preventable suffering.

Question: Is Positive Psychology responsible for the economic crisis?

Answer: Some critics blame 'positive thinking' for the current economic crisis because the market crash was based on an unswerving belief that there was never going to be an end to the economic boom. This engendered risky behaviour. To adopt this belief is to go off at an intellectual deep end. It is ludicrous to blame the housing crisis and economic problems on positive thinking. The bottom line on these issues were multiple but derived primarily from a culture of materialism that embraced easy credit, greediness, the promise of mortgages to those who could not afford them and a lack of government regulation.

Question: Is Positive Psychology illusory?

Answer: One of the major complaints centers on Positive Psychology's approval of 'positive illusions' as a means to happiness and well-being. Adherents are encouraged to 'fake it till you make' – in other words act as if you possess positive traits until they become realized.

Some would say that it is not the job of Positive Psychology to tell you that you should be optimistic, or spiritual, or kind or good-humored; it is rather to describe the consequences of these traits for physical health, and higher achievement, at a cost perhaps of less realism. If positive psychologists are dedicated to rigorous science how can they be prepared to toss out 'realism and objectivity?' Could some positive psychologists employ a 'double epistemic standard, upholding objective and unbiased science, while endorsing an 'optimistic bias' in everyday life?

Claims that work done on optimism (and Positive Psychology in general) encourages people to adopt an unrealistic perspective is emphatically false. The dangers of this manner of thinking are obvious (and, as with all good science, the hypothesis is investigated and tested nonetheless, lest we fall victim to assumptions that may turn out to be false).

The central idea in Positive Psychology is being authentic, so it means that we do recognize the negative and hard side in our lives but try to enjoy it and be happy despite of it. This is absolutely not the 'false optimism' notion that Maslow mentions. Level-headed rationality should never be trumped by wishful thinking, no matter how attractive and tempting it might be.

It is possible to do educational research with high levels of personal optimism, self-esteem and achievement and yet retain a sense of dispassionate rationality. Psychological research has demonstrated the numerous benefits of optimism, and offers tried-and-tested methods to cultivate optimism, for those to whom it may not come naturally. There is a big difference between acting with confidence that you will succeed (while being open to the feedback of your subsequent success or failure), and having your head in the clouds, subject to cognitive distortions.

Question What if the findings in one particularly study are not strong or convincing?

Answer: While respectable critics of Positive Psychology bring up valid points, these are often in regard to specific findings about particular topics within Positive Psychology, not attacks on the entire field itself. Martin Seligman said he expects that whatever spurious science gets into the mix will be eventually washed out in the normal scientific process.
My post-graduate study of research methodologies taught me that when findings are mixed, this is cause for further study, not cause for dismissing an entire field out of hand. It is important to tease out causation from mere correlation in order to avoid false conclusions, a task that can be complicated and time-consuming, but carried out nevertheless.

This represents what is best about educational research. If a finding cannot be replicated, then it is without merit. If results are unclear, then more studies and experiments ought to be done in order to clarify what is really going on. Furthermore, one single, solitary study with contradictory conclusions does not invalidate an entire hypothesis even if it cannot be replicated, and comes amidst a range of similar studies that confirm the hypothesis. Again, thoroughness in educational research is valued.

Question: It is better to be sceptical than accept these untested ideas?

Answer: In a sceptical world it is easy to remain sceptical. Some see it as intellectually admirable to be sceptical, generally speaking. It is especially understandable to view something like Positive Psychology with a little uncertainty, given its superficial similarities with the 'Positive Thinking'/Self-Help movements.

The great danger is in allowing this suspicion to descend into stubborn cynicism is a disservice to what potential Positive Psychology offers for children in the UK who are currently at the bottom of the well-being pile. At worst, a person publicly decrying Positive Psychology may discourage others from receiving the benefits of its findings.

Question: How does pursuing happiness have wider benefits?

Answer: It is possible to demonstrate that pursuing happiness may have benefits beyond simply being happy. The benefits to health, productivity, achievement, and more, that may result from being happier are not reasons unto themselves for pursuing happiness, but are welcome by-products of such happiness. It's icing on a cake that's worth eating to begin with, even without the promise of icing, since the pursuit of happiness is worthwhile in itself.

Positive Psychology is popular with educators because, some argue, if happiness is something that can be learned, it can be taught and because being happier seems to have positive long-term effects not just on well-being but also on health and life span.

Psychologists such as Langer, Seligman, Diener et al. have revealed valuable insights into what makes us truly happy (spending time with friends and family, practising gratitude, volunteering) and what doesn't. Positivity (and its cousin, optimism) has been scientifically linked to better health, less depression, and longer life. These are benefits available to everyone.

Question: How can we be positive when we all have a negativity bias?

Answer: A further complication is that psychologists draw attention to what is known as negativity bias, the name for a psychological phenomenon by which humans pay more attention to and give more weight to negative rather than positive experiences or other kinds of information. Our responses to dangers are stronger than responses to pleasure. When put in an environment with a variety of information to pay attention to, people will immediately notice the threats instead of the opportunities or the signals of safety. Evolutionary psychology sees this as an example of an early warning system.

Bad seems stronger than good. A bias to negativity can be exemplified in the way in which the media manipulates and creates anxiety so that we will pay more attention to those who forecast catastrophes than to people who make us aware of a brighter alternative. Interestingly, it was the emphasis on the psychopathologies that represent the negativity bias in psychology that caused Seligman to seek a more positive path.

Interpreting this dilemma in school settings, teachers are faced with stark choices: to actively seek the positive, or to adopt a more defensive position with a bias towards threats rather than opportunities. The former is harder work because we seem wired to find and react to setbacks.

The implications are that if we are to achieve a depth of learning with our pupils, our schools must produce the necessary conditions for psychological safety. Negative pupil emotions will be counter-productive to our best efforts. This is why a caring and kindly culture, where due regard to pupil well-being, will lead to greater pupil achievement.

Question: Have we got better things to do in schools than worry about pupil well-being lessons?

Answer: Five very cogent reasons why we must include pupil well-being lessons that are highlighted in earlier chapters of this book. We have a legal obligation to ensure that schools are meeting the Every Child Matters agenda. This is part of the Inspection process and schools have a duty to ensure that vital aspects of experience other than those prescribed by the National Curriculum are presented.

The social, moral, spiritual and cultural elements of a child's development must not be overlooked. We have to think as deeply about these areas as we do the core curriculum. This is not an either or situation. To re-iterate, the straight forward approach to effective schooling is not to falsely promote social and emotional competencies to supersede cognitive abilities but to create the schools where they re-inforce one another.

Question: Other than in school settings, can positive thinking prove a stumbling block for those with serious medical conditions?

Answer: Jimmie C. Holland, M.D., a physician and researcher who examines emotional experiences of cancer patients and their families, has written commentaries on what he calls the 'Tyranny of Positive Thinking'. He found that cancer patients, although they are going through one of the most frightening, scary, and uncertain times in their lives, feel deeply guilty if they aren't able to paint on a smiley face or find the silver lining in their experience. Some feel guilty that they aren't able to be stronger, more cheerful, and optimistic in order to comfort their families and loved ones. Others, who have read or learned somewhere that a positive outlook can perhaps help disease regression and recovery, feel guilty when they can't in fact force themselves to feel anything other than anxiety and fear through the course of their ordeal.

Consider the case of Christopher O'Brien, as discussed in the Positive Psychology literature, the world-renowned cancer specialist who died from a brain tumour. He acquired many honours during his career, including being made an officer in the Order of Australia.

Professor O'Brien, who was 57, led research into head and neck cancer in Australia and operated on hundreds of patients Diagnosed with a brain tumour in November 2006, he refused to bow to his grim prognosis. He had five major operations before succumbing to the disease in Royal Prince Alfred Hospital. He was recently rewarded for his achievement in the establishment of the $150 million Lifehouse Centre at the hospital, the first purpose-built integrated cancer centre in Australia.

Before his death, he had become paralysed on his left side, yet he retained the tenacity of mind that powered his stellar career. He seemed keen to write his own legacy. In a recent interview he stated there were three things he wanted to get across: 'The first is that I'm honoured to be recognised. Second is that, in my 30 years as a doctor and more than 20 years working as a specialist cancer surgeon, I really haven't achieved anything that was worthwhile by myself. I've been supported and assisted by many unselfish, dedicated people, the most important of whom has been my wife Gail.

He paid tribute to the Prime Minister, Kevin Rudd, for backing the cancer centre, which he believed was essential to meet the growing challenge of cancer among the ageing population.

Though his physical condition had deteriorated in the final months of his life, he was grateful he could read, and be read to by his wife and children. He said his work had prepared him for the disease and for death: 'I think inevitably I'll die of this, and I'm not frightened of dying. I'm at peace with my situation, I'm not willing it to come quick but it will come soon enough.'

This recent news piece highlights everything that Positive Psychology promotes, hard work, self-efficacy, gratitude, overcoming fear, post traumatic growth, overcoming obstacles, resilience, validation of evidence based research and the power of love.

Psycho-neuroimmunology and links with mind/body and immunity have been much researched; for example by Candace Pert (1999) who reports many cases of spontaneous remission. Would we like to deny patients the knowledge of that hope? Moreover, health care professionals can not only acknowledge patients' fears but teach strategies to work with them.

Question: Is there a link between Positive Psychology and social action?

Answer: It is possible to be an authentically happy person while also working tirelessly to right the wrongs of society. A straight taking approach says that you can be cheery and ebullient while simultaneously fighting to correct the injustices of the world. Not only is this 'paradoxical' co-existence possible, but such an individual will be more likely to succeed in helping the world than the pessimist. It is no coincidence that the people who have done the most to promote peace in the world were all optimists. King, Ghandi, and Mandela: they took action to help make it happen. The welfare state in the United Kingdom grew up to deal with physical and material needs. It evolved to provide enough food to eat, cures for sickness, homes and jobs. Now, in a society with relative material abundance, even within the conditions of austerity Britain 2012, the critical issues of welfare have become as much about psychology and relationships as about material need.

Until the end of the last century local and national policy was mostly based on clear boundaries between the fields of education, childcare and social care. Over the last decade there has been an administrative re-organisation of responsibility for children's services and a shift in how we envisage provision for children and young people.

This research points to ways in lessons in pupil well-being contributes to the possibility for 'social pedagogy', as a model, fits policy concerns for children, and the development of training and services. These are areas that present many problems for agencies across the children's services sector. Evidence shows that income has no significant bearing on our well-being and happiness with the one exception being those living in poverty. We in schools should show to pupils the necessity to fight to eliminate the scourge of poverty worldwide as well as injustice.

In fact, research shows that such a person in committing to a cause that is bigger than themselves is more likely to experience authentic happiness, the meaningful life.

Charitable work aimed at alleviating poverty and addressing social injustice is sometimes assisted by forward thinking and successful entrepreneurs who act as leaders of their generations, such as Henry Amar and the Francis Terry Trust, Jon and Sue Symonds plus colleagues at the Bujagali Trust in Uganda, Nigel Wray, Nick Leslau, Dr. Brendan Venter and the Saracens Foundation who are committed to social justice through projects such as the *Field of Dreams* (above) in Stellenbosch, South Africa and other similar charitable activities.

Conclusion:

A straightforward response to any objections would be to investigate the claims of the positive psychological approach by researching their impact in a school situation.
The next chapter is an objective review, on the basis of a six year longitudinal study, in one school in the UK that has taken the challenge of creating education for happiness seriously. It is one case study in one specific location and so clearly has many limits in terms of generalisation. The best way to measure any impact is to escape any rhetoric and false truth claims and speak to the people that matter most, the pupils themselves. Pupils have a wonderful capacity to recognise when they are being hood winked. They are forthcoming in their opinions and tend to call a spade by its true name. The results are quite surprising.

Chapter 7: Evaluating a school based, well-being curriculum.

Having discussed the scientific principles that underpin a positive psychological approach, it is now desirable to examine how these principles are put into practice in a school setting. Morris (2009) makes the very important distinction between *education as happiness* and *education for happiness*. He clearly identifies the tri-partite conditions for happiness in school settings. He argues that children are happy in schools when

1. their psychological needs are being met,
2. they enjoy and are challenged by the activities that they are engaging in and
3. when they can see reward, meaning and purpose in what they are doing.

Other commentators take a similar approach. In his book *What's the Point of School?* Guy Claxton argues that if schools were better able to help children to learn and engage with the process of learning in the first place, then education would make children happier:

> *'Happiness is better seen as a by-product of having done something challenging and worthwhile. Happiness is a mixture of pride, satisfaction and the sense of effectiveness and value that arises when we have stretched ourselves to achieve something we care about. In other words, happiness is the fruit of worthwhile learning. In my view, too much stress and unhappiness in young people's lives comes from the fact that they do not know how to learn, nor what it is that they want to learn about. If we can help them to discover the things they most passionately want to get better at, and to develop the confidence and capability to pursue those passions, then I think more happiness and less stress will be the result.'*
>
> Claxton, 2008

Simply described, schools have a twofold role in the promotion of happiness. Firstly, the school itself must be a happy place to be. The basic needs of the pupils need to be met, the curriculums (formal, informal and hidden) must enable pupils to discover and develop their physical, intellectual and social strengths and abilities and above all, the school must create the conditions for excellence and allow its pupils to discover a sense of meaning and purpose that will carry them well beyond the school gates. This might be termed *'education as happiness.'*

Secondly, schools should give explicit guidance to their pupils on how happiness might be achieved in life and not just assume that happiness will result from the ordinary activities of school life; this might be termed *'educating for happiness.'* It is this second suggested role that is controversial and that has attracted a great deal of media attention in recent times. Here is a description of this approach by Morris (2009) :

'Educating for happiness

As mentioned above, happiness education involves not only helping young people to be happy as they learn, but helping them to learn how to make themselves happier. Since 2006, we have been pioneering lessons in happiness at Wellington College. From their arrival and for the first three years they are at Wellington, all students receive discrete happiness lessons. The aim of our course is to put students in touch with the wealth of research that has gone into what causes human flourishing, and to give them the opportunity to put the fruits of this research to the test in their own lives. Our happiness lessons focus on what it means to be a human being, what our students can do to make the best of their human resources and most importantly, what it might mean to lead a flourishing life. In this way, alongside the provision of a well-delivered formal curriculum, a varied programme of extra-curricular activities, and the pastoral care provided by a boarding environment, happiness lessons join up *education as happiness* with *educating for happiness*.

Sometimes education of this sort (traditionally called something like Personal Social and Health Education in the UK) descends either into lessons in prohibition where adults tell children what harmful things not to do; or they begin with a fabulous list of concepts, but with none of the conceptual underpinning or practical application that would enable students to do something with them, leaving students with a cosy chat about feelings which effects no change. For us, the lessons firstly had to be aspirational: guidance on how life ought to be lived and secondly, practical, providing real guidance on how to flourish based on reliable research, rather than bad science. Clearly, there is a need to signpost students to particular dangerous activities such as substance abuse and unsafe sex, and commentators such as Barbara Ehrenreich (2009) have lambasted those who advocate positivity at all costs and ignore obvious dangers citing this as a cause of amongst other things, the economic downturn caused by the collapse of the sub-prime property market. I agree with this criticism, but also take note of the work of researchers such David Cooperrider who cautions against excessive focus on the negative in trying to effect change and Martin Seligman who talks about flourishing not as a removal of ills but as a promotion of goods.

Mindfulness

Each lesson begins with some mindfulness meditation. Research has shown that people who meditate regularly can have:

- increased activity in their cerebral cortex
- increased resistance to disease
- a stronger capacity to deal with the stresses and strains of life.

The other thing we do is something called counting blessings. Research shows that people engage more fully with life and have a generally higher level of well-being if they:

- count their blessings regularly
- say thank you
- are grateful for the things that happen to them on a daily basis.

In this way, we teach our students to be grateful for the things that happen to them.

Biographical learning

We do a lot of biographical learning, looking at the lives of other people and seeing what the ingredients of a happy life are. We might use film clips as a stimulus. Ken Loach's early film, 'Kes', for example, shows various examples of well-being. We use a variety of techniques to teach young people how to:

- manage their anger
- resolve conflict
- act out the mental processes they will need to go through to get their neo-cortex working to get them out of these intense emotional states.

For me, the aim is to equip the young people with the skills they will need to live life successfully. We want to make them more self-aware and resilient so as to help them to flourish as human beings. '

The methodology

Each one hour lesson follows a similar structure, set out graphically below:

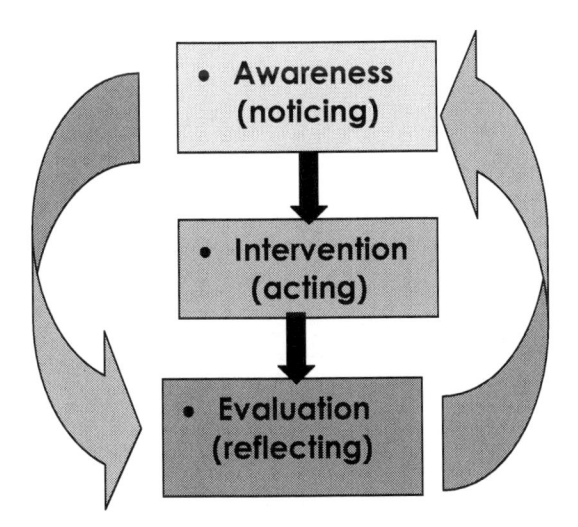

- **Awareness (noticing)**
- **Intervention (acting)**
- **Evaluation (reflecting)**

A typical lesson begins with 'awareness', something to bring the lesson topic to life for the students; this could be anything from a short video clip to a game or even just a question or a picture; something to capture the interest of the students and that will provoke discussion and the sharing of ideas and the asking of questions. Once the students are on board with the topic, the awareness continues by enhancing their understanding of a particular aspect of being human. This may involve looking at (or perhaps rehearsing) a psychological experiment that reveals aspects of human nature or looking at somebody else's experiences and comparing them with our own.

We then move into the 'intervention' part of the lesson, where the students learn a specific skill that might help them to maximise their happiness: for example, in the lessons on physical health (described below), students learn techniques to help them sleep, advice on how to maximise learning or ways of managing stress. It is important that students have the opportunity to try the interventions out together and learn through experience. It is all too easy to just tell students 'if you want to achieve X, then do Y' but unless students have an opportunity to try these ideas out with guidance when needed, the interventions simply won't get used by them.

The third section of the lesson, 'evaluation', is where we encourage the students to evaluate the intervention they have just learned and they do this in between the lessons. All students are provided with a happiness journal where they write down their reflections on the usefulness of the interventions we teach, or keep notes on how what they are learning in the lessons is impacting upon their subjective well-being. This element of the methodology is vital, because it offers the students the opportunity to provide reasons why they accept or *reject* what they have learned. Happiness is ultimately subjective and the activities that we choose to engage in to promote our own happiness have to have subjective value based on individual reasoning. The more prescriptive and dictatorial we become about happiness, the more we undermine the validity of what we are doing.

Course content: the six strands.

Our course is divided up into 6 strands which we believe cover the range of knowledge of the causes of human flourishing, deriving from disciplines such as the human sciences, Psychology, Philosophy and Theology. The strands are as follows:

1. Physical health.
2. Positive relationships.
3. Perspective: building psychological capital.
4. Strengths.
5. The world: learning to live sustainably in a consumer culture.
6. Meaning and purpose.

There is insufficient room to go into comprehensive detail for each strand, but what follows will give a sense of what is taught and the justifications for teaching it.

The course begins with 'Physical Health' and an examination of the physical factors that can help to promote flourishing. Lessons in this strand look at basic care of the physical self through sensible diet, sleep and exercise and build on common knowledge in these areas by introducing the students to research that they may not be familiar with by people such as Bernard Gesch, who has studied the effect of nutrition on young offender and by John Ratey who has written extensively on the benefits of exercise for combating low mood and improving learning and creativity in his books *Spark* and *A User's Guide to the Brain*. This strand also devotes time to exploring exactly what happens in the brain when we learn (and contains a lovely lesson where students make neuronal connections with modelling clay) and how to resist temptation. The lesson on learning aims to emphasise the idea of neuro-plasticity to the students as well as giving them practical advice on how to maximise their chances of learning. Many young people fall into the trap of thinking that learning ability is fixed by genetics, and it is important to show them just how powerful the effect of behaviours such as exercise, diet and sleep is on learning. The lesson on resisting temptation fits in with recent work on delayed gratification and executive function, and gives students advice on how to use incentives and distractions to try to resist unhelpful temptations.

Students learn:

- how to improve the way their mind works through the way they manage their bodies
- how to manage their subconscious mind and be aware of how it can influence the conscious mind
- how simply being out in the natural world can increase their well-being
- that it is not good to immerse themselves in the fantasy world of television and video games
- how to resolve conflict with others
- the benefits of stillness and mindfulness meditation.

The second strand, 'Positive Relationships' looks at techniques for the better management of relationships, with a focus on experiential learning. For example, trust is explored using games from drama; altruism and gratitude are explored by practising random acts of kindness and keeping a gratitude journal; attentiveness is explored by trying out Active Constructive Responding, and long term relationships are considered using a charity called *Explore*, who bring married couples into schools to talk about their experiences of being in a long term relationship. This strand also pays attention to emotional recognition and management.

The third strand, 'Perspective' provides students with strategies to help them successfully adapt and function in the face of challenge or trauma: in short, building resilience and grit, or what Daniel Gilbert (2006) has called the *'psychological immune system'*. So many of us are hampered by our thinking patterns and this unit owes its existence to the brilliant insights of people such as Aaron Beck, Martin Seligman and Carol Dweck, who not only describe how our thoughts and misperceptions can limit us but also offer us practical strategies for overcoming those limitations. Perspective lessons cover techniques such as getting an accurate perspective on events and challenging unhelpful patterns of thinking, challenging the 'fixed mindset' view that ability and talent is the result of genetics by emphasising neuro-plasticity, the role of effort in achievement and self-efficacy beliefs. We bring these cognitive ideas to life with stories such as Aesop's fable of the hare and the tortoise, Roald Dahl's story of Fantastic Mr Fox, exploding super-hero myths surrounding the athlete Usain Bolt or looking at how climber Joe Simpson overcame enormous adversity to survive a horrendous climbing accident. Lessons in perspective are complemented by the teaching of Philosophy, which similarly attempts to develop an accurate perspective on the world.

The fourth strand, 'Strengths' really goes to the heart of the purpose of education, which is to discover and draw out our best selves. In this unit, students explore how to discover and nurture character strengths and abilities using the VIA Signature Strengths Inventory, and also look at the research of Mihaly Csikszentmihalyi into optimal psychological states.. Again, in these lessons the emphasis is upon the experiential and the reflective: one of the most powerful strengths lessons is where students talk to each other about times when they have used their character strengths, in other words where they get to talk about being at their best, which sadly is often a rarity in schools as our target setting and exam result culture often has them skip over achievement to focus on areas of weakness, which are given undue weight.

The fifth strand, 'The World' looks at how to survive in a culture which tends to advocate conspicuous consumerism at the expense of more sustainable forms of living. Here we rely on suggestions made by Barry Schwartz and Oliver James on how to resist the consumer culture and by an organisation called *Adbusters* on how to be more media critical. This strand also explores how the beauty of the natural and man-made world can be used to elevate us.

The course finishes by spending time reflecting on meaning and purpose and this moment comes just before the students are due to sit their first series of major public examinations and start to make decisions about directions in life. This unit takes its inspiration from Viktor Frankl, who in *Man's Search for Meaning* suggests that there is no one meaning of life, but that it is down to the individual to find and express their own meaning and purpose. We spend time looking at what life might hold for the students (using the Eriksonian structure found in George Vaillant's work (2003)), what skills they will need to bring about their own flourishing and how what they know of themselves so far can help to carry them there.'

Summary: The Wellington Well-Being Course.: well-being lessons are currently taught to students in Years 9 to 11 (pupils aged 14-16 years). The course is based upon strands of well-being, which are as follows:

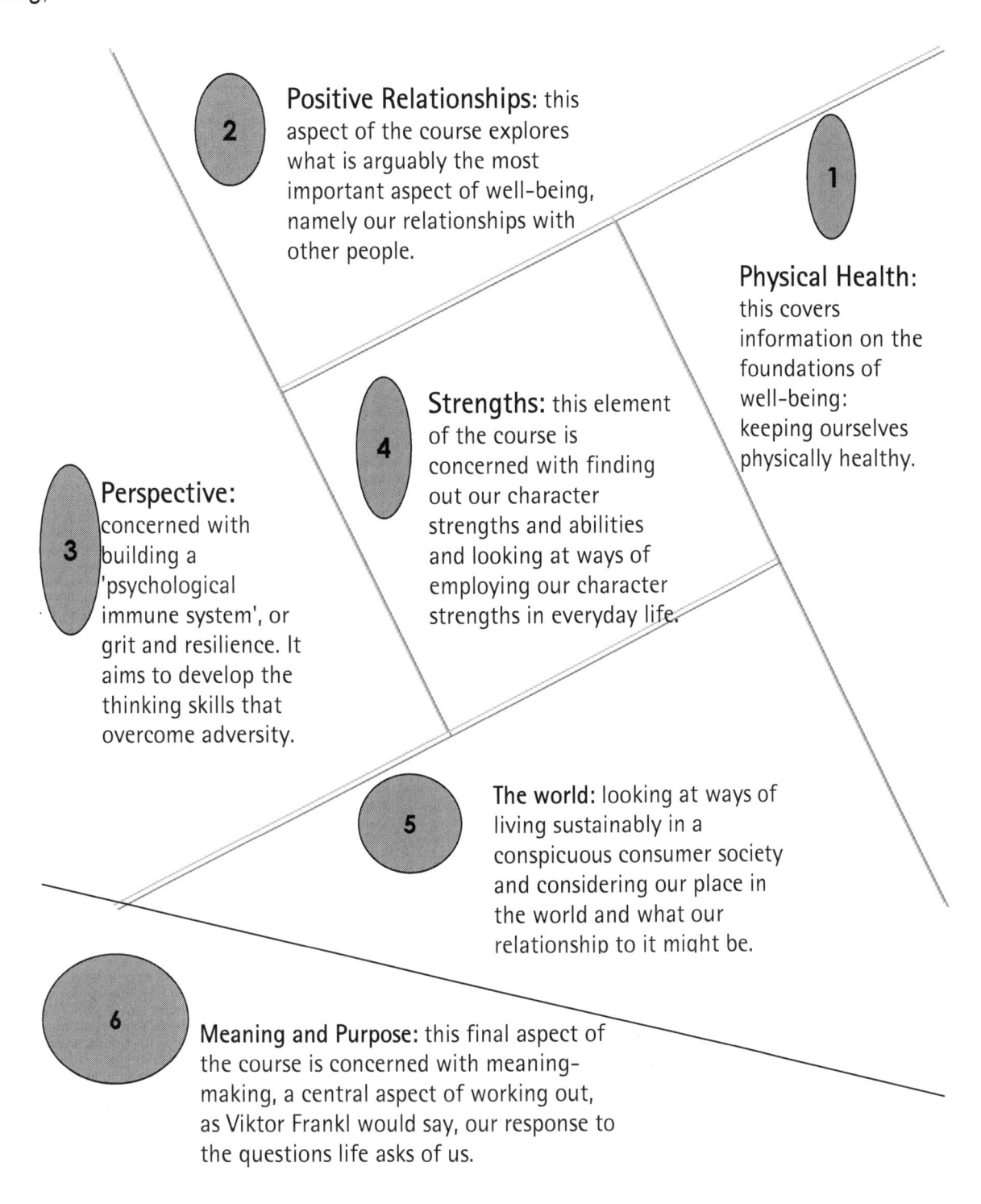

2 Positive Relationships: this aspect of the course explores what is arguably the most important aspect of well-being, namely our relationships with other people.

1 Physical Health: this covers information on the foundations of well-being: keeping ourselves physically healthy.

4 Strengths: this element of the course is concerned with finding out our character strengths and abilities and looking at ways of employing our character strengths in everyday life.

3 Perspective: concerned with building a 'psychological immune system', or grit and resilience. It aims to develop the thinking skills that overcome adversity.

5 The world: looking at ways of living sustainably in a conspicuous consumer society and considering our place in the world and what our relationship to it might be.

6 Meaning and Purpose: this final aspect of the course is concerned with meaning-making, a central aspect of working out, as Viktor Frankl would say, our response to the questions life asks of us.

Staff perspectives

An area that has been researched more in the last decade is the relationship between social support, feelings of emotional well-being or distress, and teacher-pupil relationships. Roeser et al (2000) in concluding a meta review wrote,

> *'The theoretical argument is straightforward: to the extent that adolescents perceive teacher and school staff as providing them with opportunities to develop their academic and social competencies, to exercise autonomous control over aspects of their learning and to feel care and supported during learning, adolescents' perceptions of their academic competence, their valuing of school and their emotional well-being should all be enhanced.'* (p.458)

McLaughlin and Clarke (2010) remind us that the role of relationships with teachers and pupils is central to engagement:

> *'When exploring the key factors in motivation and success at school, relationships with teachers emerge as central and play a particular part in emotional well-being (Wentzel, 1998: Roeser et al, 2000: Weare and Gray, 2003). Wentzel argues that social support is a key variable for all pupils, not just vulnerable or minority groups. She also warns against generalising to all age groups as she feels that middle school pupils are a particular group.'*

Other recent UK research (Mayall, 2007) has emphasised young adolescents' desire for positive pupil-teacher relationships. As Rudduck and Flutter (2004) have argued, what was striking about teachers identified by young people as 'good' was that 'the qualities that mattered to pupils tended to be as much about how they were *treated* as how they were taught'. So academic outcomes, social support, and relationships are deeply interconnected.

Bowlby (1969) argued that an attachment figure was an essential component to mental well-being:

> *'human beings of all ages are happiest and able to deploy their talents to best advantage when they are confident that, standing behind them, there are one or more trusted persons who will come to their aid should difficulties arise'*

The sense of belonging that can arise from an emotional connection to individuals within the school, including peers and teachers, is fundamental to the sense of connectedness. It has been recognised that teacher-pupil relationships are a significant factor (McLaughlin and Clarke, 2010). Over the last decade reviews of research have acknowledged the central role and importance of teacher-pupil relationships to emotional well-being in schools (Durlak and Wells, 1997; Weare and Gray, 2003).

Many of these theoretical propositions are echoed in the words of the respondents in this book.

Teacher 1 writes:

'Celebrity, money and possessions are too often the touchstones for teenagers, and yet these are not where happiness lies. Helping our students understand this, and learn what really contributes to a sense of personal contentment and well-being, lies behind ..... the decision to teach the 'skills of well-being' (colloquially called 'happiness lessons'). This has sparked enormous- and unexpected - national and international interest.

We know that parents want their children to be happy at school above anything else, even exam results. Indeed, happy children do better at exams than stressed children, and develop into more successful adults. Bringing in lessons in Positive Psychology and well-being is a natural evolution of our philosophy of educating the whole child. We developed the happiness course with Dr Nick Baylis, a psychologist at Cambridge University. The basic principle behind the lessons is that we can learn the skills of living well. This is not new. Aristotle wrote about it in the Nichomachean Ethics. And the discipline of Positive Psychology is teaching us this as well, with empirical evidence to back it up.

It should be obvious that a student will not be able to access the curriculum effectively if there are barriers to learning in their lives. We all arrive at school carrying our own emotional, psychological, social and physical issues with us. When these issues are unresolved, they cause us problems and throw up barriers to progress. If we can teach our students the skills that will enable them to start overcoming these barriers, they will be better equipped to access the curriculum.

The course is aimed at students in Years 10 and 11. It is designed to show them that life is something to be lived skillfully, and that there are certain skills which they can learn and employ to make their lives go better.

Students' perspectives

In 2005 the *Good Childhood Inquiry* surveyed around 8,000 14-16 year olds from across the UK (Pople, 2009: 17-18). McLaughlin and Clarke (2010) demonstrate effectively that the survey reports that children often 'spontaneously mentioned' school and education when asked about 'the ingredients of a good life'. What young people valued highly was time with friends from whom they derived 'intimacy, support and pleasure'. The absence of such friendships was felt keenly by a minority. Equally valued was having 'good teachers' who were 'kind and supportive' 'passionate about their subjects' and who made lessons 'interesting and fun'. They were also concerned about bullying and the 'disruptive behaviour of other pupils'. Exams and schoolwork were also a source of stress. So young people perceived school as playing a role in well-being. The factors mentioned by the pupils convey a strong sense of the school as a social institution where the social experiences referred to by Rutter (1991) emerge as important. This is borne out by the reports of pupil respondents in this book:

> *'When the school's well-being campaign launched, we were all a bit sceptical. We thought the new master was just doing it to look good. Happiness lessons seemed an unlikely proposition. How could we be taught to be happy? We had already sat through PSHE and citizenship. We had this vision of getting a D mark for being gloomy or the occasional pubescent mood swing.*

But our happiness lessons are actually well-being lessons. That is an important distinction. Because you can't teach someone to be happy, you can only teach them to pretend to be happy. And, if they are only pretending to be happy that is no use to anyone. What the school is trying to do is give us some sort of basis, so that when we have a time of sadness or grief, we can deal with it constructively rather than turn to false comforts of drugs and alcohol.

It is easy to get trapped in unhealthy relationships. What enables you to step out of them is your own self-worth and individuality.

There is also a much more practical aspect. I know a lot of people use meditation to help them go to sleep. Small things like that can make a big difference to your day. An extra hour's sleep can really impact on your learning.

It comes across in different ways for different people. You get out what you put in. What you get out is different for everyone. It helps you objectify what you are doing and be more constructive in your learning.'

Pupil A

'For me, the purpose of the lessons is to instil some values that we will keep with us; so that when a difficult time comes around, we make better decisions.

Our culture is dominated by advertisements about wealth, cars, and the happiness which material possessions offer. This provokes feelings of inadequacy and a general view that, in order to be happy, you must be rich. We have lost contact with the meaning of true happiness, which goes hand in hand with overall well-being.

These lessons bring us back to the roots of living a healthy and productive life. So what if you have failed the test or you didn't get into the university that you wanted? If you are happy with your surroundings, and with the people around you, you don't have to be hard on yourself.'

Pupil B

Survey Data.

Much important data has been collected from senior school pupils in the UK. 'Tell us' is a national survey which gathers children and young people's views on their life, their school and their local area. This methodology was influential in terms of the research design for this small scale project. Accordingly, an instrument was designed to collect data from pupils about their views. A random sample of 52 pupils completed a pupil well-being survey that comprised a Likert scale to measure five essential elements of the pupil well-being programme, namely pupil enjoyment, relevance of material studied, resilience, thinking skills /mindfulness as well as any self-reported behavioural change. Direct evidence here is provided by surveys of self-reports on verbal scales that might have different meanings depending on the language and culture in which they were written. At this point, however, they represent the state of the art in research in the UK independent schools sector, an art that will inevitably become more precise with time.

1060 items of data were collected from 52 respondents over a period of a week through a pupil survey. The five essential elements were measured with a maximum score being twenty out of twenty for a strong positive correlation.

Enjoyment

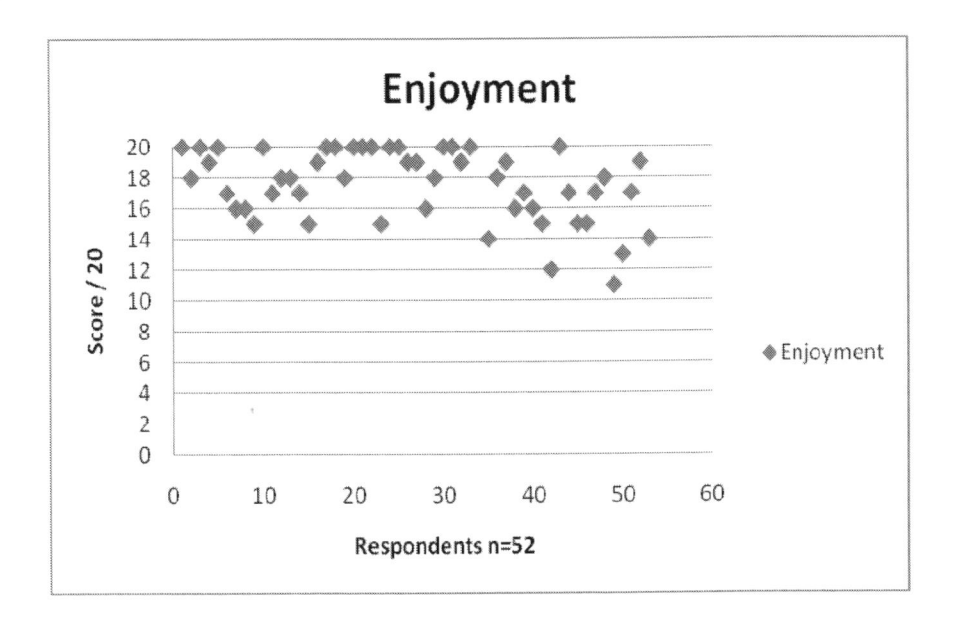

[Scatter plot titled "Enjoyment" showing Score / 20 on y-axis (0-20) against Respondents n=52 on x-axis (0-60), with enjoyment data points mostly clustered between scores of 14-20.]

Enjoyment refers to Csikszentmihalyi's notion of optimal experience or flow as the experience of intense involvement that is willingly enacted, psychologically absorbing, and ultimately satisfying.

While enjoyment and associated functional development stand well as outcomes and as indicators of self-determination, they are also a precipitating experience. Thus, enjoyment and associated functional improvements serve to reinforce experiences and lead a person on to greater challenges and to higher levels of self-determination. As enjoyment reflects control by the individual, it evokes an orientation for making the most of circumstances and can result in improved physical, social, emotional, and cognitive functioning.

The assessment of achievement and enjoyment of lessons is one of the key judgements made by the inspectorate in UK schools: enjoyment is a key indicator of pupil well-being outcomes for the Office for Standards in Education (Leeson 2009). Lessons in well-being are received well and can be succinctly summarised in the words of Pupil1

> 'the relaxing mood in the lessons which helps you to learn
> and enjoy what you are learning'

A repeated theme in the pupil questionnaires was the different mood or tone of the lessons:

> 'The lessons offer a welcome break from the rigours of academic work. Having a timetabled lesson in which you, as a pupil, know that you can relax and be yourself is a relief. You can take your mind off work and learn something about yourself for a change'.

The vast majority of pupils scored very highly on questions relating to enjoyment of lessons and all looked forward to the next session. One of very few comments that could be regarded as negative expressed by four pupils was a plea for increased frequency as there is only one session per fortnight currently.

Meaning

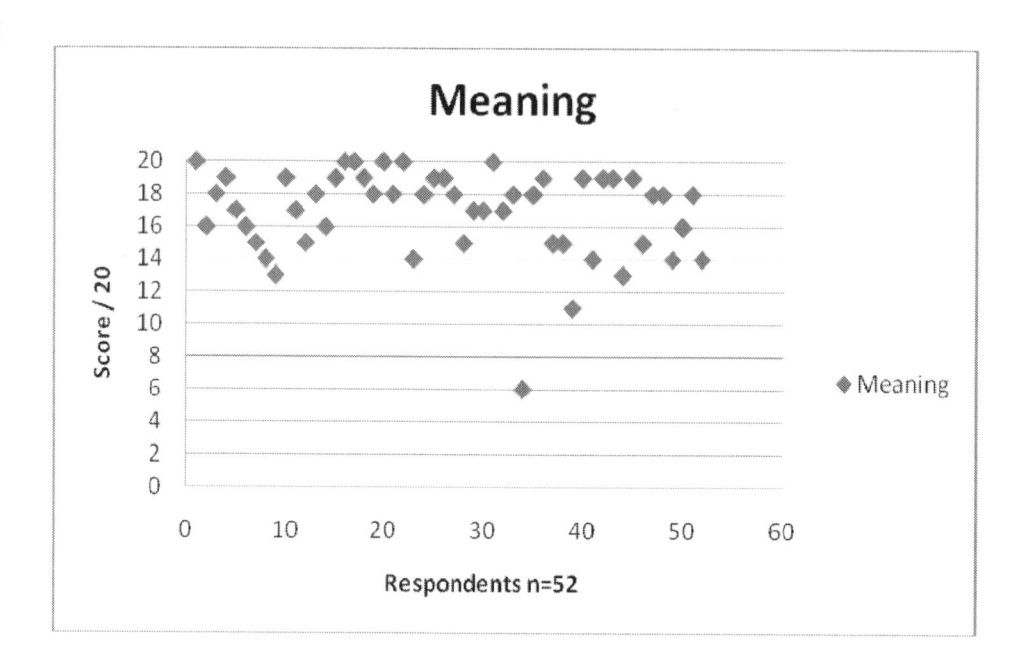

Meaning scatter plot: Score / 20 vs Respondents n=52

The sense of engagement that the respondents experience in these lessons was very evident in the data. This is a reflection of the time and energy spent in planning the sessions so that they are relevant to the life experiences of the pupils. Sociologist Glen Elder also provides an interesting insight into the social aspects of meaning making:

> 'There is a storyline across all the work I have done. Events do not have meaning in themselves. Those meanings are derived from the interactions between people groups and the experience itself.'

Social networks developed in supportive and creative educational environments offer avenues for finding meaning and purpose. Five pupils made a point of commenting that the material covered in lessons was both interesting and relevant e.g.

'The topics are relevant (of) what I am going through.'
                                                                Pupil 4
'The subjects we do I can relate to'
                                                                Pupil 16

'they are helpful for life in general'

Pupil 24

'the thing I appreciate about well-being lessons is interesting subjects'
Pupil 27

This is an interesting finding in the light of initial comments in this book that suggested the subject matter in the realm of social, moral spiritual or cultural education has to be in some way controversial or contain popular appeal to be of any interest to young adults.

Resilience

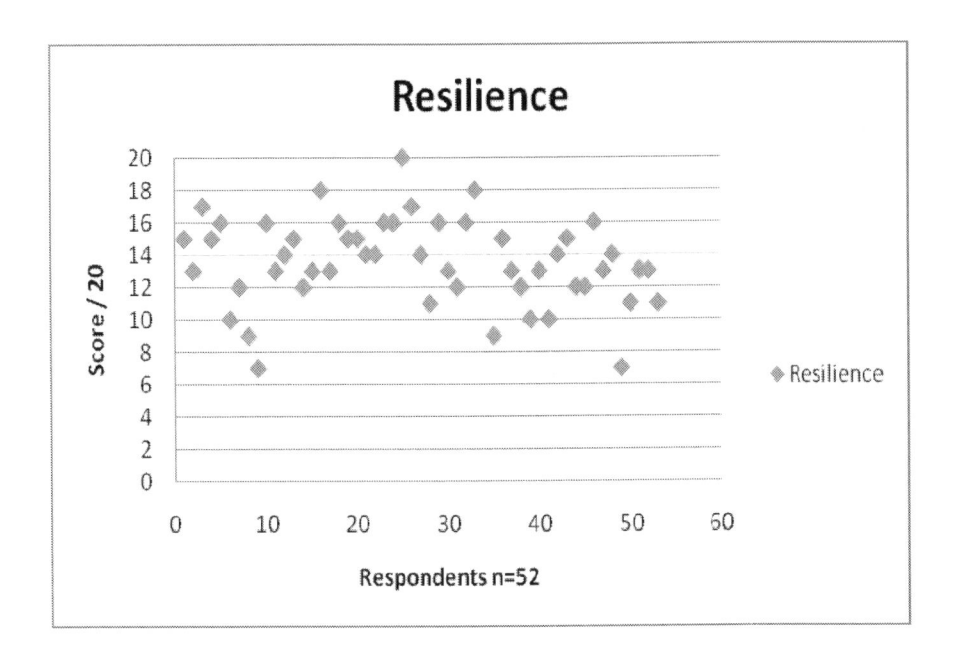

<chart: Resilience scatter plot, Score / 20 vs Respondents n=52>

Resilience matters and can be influenced. Education authorities in South Tyneside, Hertfordshire, and Manchester have already introduced resilience classes into the school curriculum. Wellington College takes the teaching of resilience seriously. The rationale is that everyone is bound to face shocks and setbacks at some point in life, but what makes the difference is how well we cope with these shocks, how well we bounce back. Society's ability to meet people's psychological and psycho-social needs appears to have declined. The buffers of religion and family that helped people cope with setbacks have weakened. There has been a rise of individualism. A more overtly meritocratic society has encouraged people to be more ambitious for themselves, but also made them more vulnerable to failure – and more likely to blame themselves if things go wrong. This creates a particular need to help promote a sense of resilience to the pressures of everyday life. This is, in part, a matter of social support from family and friends, teachers or GPs, as well as skills. This kind of discipline and resilience – and psychological fitness in a broader sense – can also be learned, and enhanced.

There is a growing body of scientific evidence on the causal factors around happiness and well-being, which can then be applied in work with individuals and institutions. Having a better understanding of how to increase the likelihood of happiness with life, and how to channel the emotional pains of set-backs en route, are the sort of skills that can substantially improve an individual's progress. Seligman's work in combating depression in young people through his Penn Resiliency Programme has had remarkable effects: 17 studies found that after 30 months, students of the programme were half as likely to show behavioural problems as those who had not taken part in the course.

A sample scheme of work is included here:

'The Psychological Immune System

It's all very well building up our physical health, but if we are psychologically unhealthy we can find ourselves right back at square one, especially because much of what happens in our mind directly affects our physical health. At the same time as trying to develop physical health, we should be trying our best to develop our psychological health and build up our psychological immunity so that we can deal with the slings and arrows of life.

In the same way that the physical immune system is strengthened when it has a disease to fight, so the psychological immune system is strengthened by challenge, struggle and overcoming adversity. Psychological immunity is not about escape, it is about engagement.

You will learn 5 techniques that will help you to build up your psychological immunity:

1. **ABC:** this helps you to spot your patterns of thinking when you encounter a difficult situation.
2. **Put it in Perspective:** this helps you to get a grip on reality and stop your thoughts getting carried away with themselves.
3. **Mindset:** this helps you to remember that the main ingredient in being successful at something is effort, rather than natural talent.
4. **Self-efficacy:** this is our belief in our ability to change things in our life: a main ingredient of psychological health is the belief that we can change things.
5. **Post-traumatic Growth:** seeing adversity as an opportunity to grow and develop rather than languish and wither.'

The benefits are described by pupil B

> 'The happiness programme has given me a better understanding of how to control pressure. The meditation techniques we learn help me to calm my nerves, whether before an important sporting fixture or an academic examination'.

The survey results again demonstrate a strongly positive response to statements such as 'well-being lessons help me to deal positively with troubles in my life' and 'well-being lessons help me to see that good things can come out of bad experiences'

Mindfulness, relaxation and calm thinking

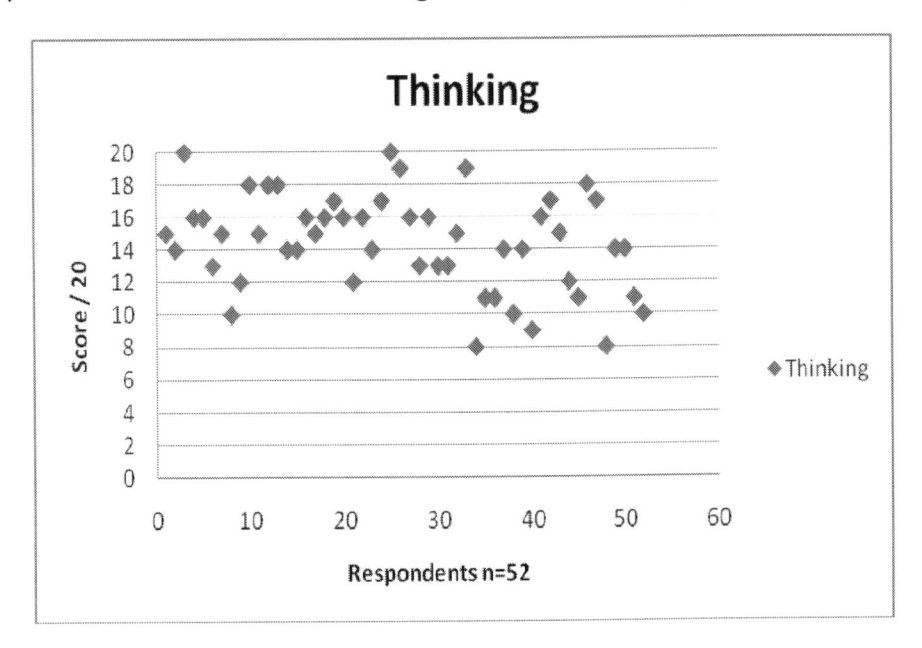

Thinking

[Scatter plot: Score / 20 (y-axis, 0 to 20) vs Respondents n=52 (x-axis, 0 to 60), showing Thinking data points]

Teacher A comments 'Teaching Mindfulness has been a feature of the well-being programme at school since it began in 2006. It is an ancient practice which simply requires one to attend to the present moment, rather than allowing one's mind to flit between past present and future. There are many things that can be used as a focus for mindfulness, from the breath to walking, from sounds in the world around us to sensations in our body.

Research over the last few years has made a strong connection between mindfulness and happiness. It seems that those who meditate regularly exhibit higher levels of activity in the left pre-frontal cortex of the brain, which is associated with positive emotion. There is also a proposed connection between mindfulness and creativity. Tal ben Shahar suggests that even three deep, well-taken breaths can start off a virtuous cycle of calm and begin to undo feelings of anxiety.'

Pupil A comments: 'There is also a much more practical aspect. I know a lot of people use meditation to help them go to sleep. Small things like that can make a big difference to your day. An extra hour's sleep can really impact on your learning'.

The majority of pupils scored high to moderately high in answer to statements such as 'well-being lessons help me to become more thoughtful and understanding' and 'well-being lessons encourage me to become calmer in my thinking'. Many pupils use the mindfulness element of the course to reduce stress; others use it before dramatic, musical or sporting performances to enhance their focus; others because of they enjoy a sense of peace and tranquility that it brings.

Acquisition of new skills / Perceived Behavioural Change

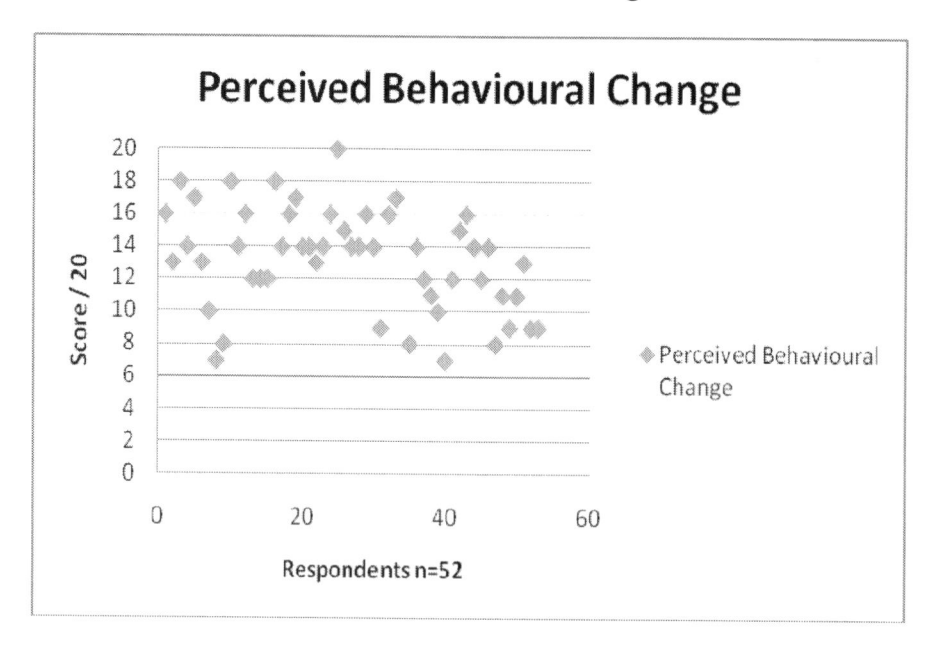

Perceived Behavioural Change

[Scatter plot: Score /20 (y-axis, 0–20) vs Respondents n=52 (x-axis, 0–60), showing Perceived Behavioural Change data points mostly ranging between 7 and 19.]

Teaching well-being is conducted with the aim of achieving behavioural change.

Teacher A explains his methodology:

'A typical well-being lesson begins with 'awareness, something to bring the lesson topic to life for the students; this could be anything from a short video clip to a game or even just a question or a picture; something to capture the interest of the students and that will provoke discussion and the sharing of ideas and the asking of questions. Once the students are on board with the topic, the awareness continues by enhancing their understanding of a particular aspect of being human. This may involve looking at (or perhaps rehearsing) a psychological experiment that reveals aspects of human nature or looking at somebody else's experiences and comparing them with our own. One of our students' favourite lessons involves re-enacting Walter Mischel's famous delayed gratification experiment where they have to employ strategies to resist jelly babies (instead of marshmallows) for the lesson.

We then move into the 'intervention' part of the lesson, where the students learn a specific skill that might help them to maximise their happiness: for example, in the lessons on physical health (described below), students learn techniques to help them sleep, advice on how to maximise learning or ways of managing stress. It is important that students have the opportunity to try the interventions out together and learn through experience. It is all too easy to just tell students 'if you want to achieve X, then do Y' but unless students have an opportunity to try these ideas out with guidance when needed, the interventions simply won't get used by them.

The third section of the lesson, 'evaluation', is where we encourage the students to evaluate the intervention they have just learned and they do this in between the lessons. All students are provided with a happiness journal where they write down their reflections on the usefulness of the interventions we teach, or keep notes on how what they are learning in the lessons is impacting upon their subjective well-being. This element of the methodology is vital, because it offers the students the opportunity to provide reasons why they accept or *reject* what they have learned. Happiness is ultimately subjective and the activities that we choose to engage in to promote our own happiness have to have subjective value based on individual reasoning. The more prescriptive and dictatorial we become about happiness the more we undermine the validity of what we are doing.'

It is appropriate to discuss at this point whether well-beings lessons are merely instructional in effect as opposed to being transformational, in terms of pupil behavioural outcomes. A range of behavioural changes have been reported in this survey. As pupil A explains:

> *'What difference has it made? Part of what we pick up is that some things are just not that important. That allows you to think about things objectively and say if I don't do really well in it, it is not going to be the end, it doesn't mean I am rubbish at this subject. That allows you to be less stressed about it and actually do better in the subject because of it.'*

The data for the final section offer more variety of response than the other four categories, with a fifth of the sample reporting moderate behavioural change, perhaps reflecting the complexity of the task required which was to reflect on the antecedents for behaviour. Statements included 'my well-being lessons have helped me change my behaviour for the better' and 'well-being lessons have helped me to remain positive when faced with difficulties'.

We must avoid the dangers of monism, an example of which is that all human motivation can be explained by only one antecedent (Seligman 2011). I am not trying to extrapolate the most impact from the fewest variables for the sake of simplicity, although the Aristotelian maxim that the actions we take are done in order for us to become happier has a seductive appeal. The data here suggest that simple interventions can assist pupils to change their affective style. The evidence from Wellington is that pupils report many benefits as a result of these well-being classes and it is time that efforts are taken to extend the benefits of this approach, even if the results from this individual study are provisional and cannot be generalized. What can be said is that it is time to give more practical attention to the well-being of our pupils at a time when high stakes testing has dominated the educational agenda at a very great cost.

Chapter 8 : Conclusions

Lord of the Flies?

I was fortunate enough recently to attend a high quality training day for educational leaders, led by some interesting speakers who had many illuminating and astute things to say about the current challenges facing educationalists in austerity Britain. Well-known author, historian and controversial TV presenter David Starkey was recently afforded a unique opportunity when offered a chance to play the role of teacher in Jamie Oliver's Dream School experiment. The premise here was to give some teenagers, who had previously been unsuccessful in their school careers for a host of reasons, a second chance by providing the very best teaching and resources available. This was a chance to engage in a social experiment that a bone fide educational researcher could only fantasise about.

The conclusions of David Starkey were quite illuminating:

> *'Education might be at the centre of our political debate, but I realise now that until you have stood in front of a class and tried to teach in this kind of challenging environment, you don't know much about the realities. The programme hasn't necessarily offered solutions, but it has highlighted the problems we face. And it does provide incontrovertible evidence to show why a lack of discipline is at the root of our educational malaise.*
>
> *I have nothing but contempt for the new-style head teachers who adopt a 'happy family' approach, where everything is laid back. It has failed several generations already – and now society is paying the consequences. Jamie's restaurants are run like military operations: why aren't our schools?*
>
> *And how could we really save the children in Jamie's school? I would prescribe a good dollop of discipline – and a system of one-to-one mentoring. I am sure this would work wonders.'*

David Starkey on Jamie's Dream School   *The Daily Telegraph,* 19.2.11

Despite having been given the golden opportunity to show that material resources are the panacea to the educational challenges in the UK and that an unlimited budget could cure all educational ills, Starkey was able to demonstrate quite quickly that, at the heart of all good teaching, is a sense of rapport between teachers and taught. Initially he went about alienating elements of his class by passing inappropriate comments that added significantly to the friction in the classroom.

Starkey reached the conclusion that 'new style' headteachers are not only contemptible but fully responsible for the creaking education system.

I respectfully disagree with Prof. Starkey on two counts. Firstly he subscribes fully to a William Golding view of child psychology (in' Lord of the Flies') in which schools become an enactment of natural selection principles and mercy and tolerance are conspicuous by their absence. These are the schools that we sang along with Roger Waters about in the 70s. If left to their own devices, pupils, in Starkey's schema, ignored by psychopathic pedagogues, would simply engage in bullying and violent tactics that would lead to fratricide. I think we owe our pupils better than this simplistic expectation.

Secondly, he overemphasizes, in my view, the belief that you have to be a weak leader to offer a pastoral alternative – to play at 'happy families' - other than a strict regimen of core curricular subjects. It is not an either or option. **To re-iterate, the straight forward approach to effective schooling is not to promote social and emotional competancies to supercede cognitive abilities, but to create the schools where they re-inforce one another.** Sadly, Jamie's 'Dream School' experiment failed in this respect.

Where Starkey was right, however, was when he identified the efficacy of a system of 'one to one mentoring' – we might call this a personalised approach to learning - where teachers manage to achieve a meaningful, professional relationship with their pupils. We have to create environments where children want to learn and where they can discover their passions. We have to use our creativity to transform our education system by personalising it, building on the achievements of the pupils and discovering the individual talents of our children.

The key message of this book is that we need to focus on strengths in schools so that our pupils can really discover their passion, enthusiasms and signature strengths so that they can realize their potential. The truth is that this will not always be found in the academic subjects, however attractive this idea might become in a world dominated by measuring success in the core subjects. We have to be realistic enough to realise that not all children are polymaths. The beauty of the type of well-being syllabus described here is that it provides more opportunities for children to find fulfilment and happiness as opposed to a narrow assessment on the basis of score in standardised tests at key stages.

Sir Ken Robinson (2009) has succinctly highlighted why the current model of schools and schooling is failing. Based on a Victorian, industrial paradigm, our schools continue to act out an assembly line model, where teachers segment knowledge into subjects, with some teachers installing maths, others history etc. There are standard units of time that are announced, factory like, with a loud bell or buzzer. Children are taught in batches according to their date of manufacture. Pupils are measured in standardised tests before being sent out into the market place for their working hours to be auctioned off, usually to the highest bidder.

Do we subscribe to a standardisation – some call it a McDonald's model of schooling - where everything looks the same as a way of trying to protect standards but in doing so create a product that is intrinsically bad for children? Should we not be adopting a Michelin star, individual model where schools reflect perfectly their context and respond with a bespoke product that serve the children's best efforts?
What is interesting in this interpretation is the way in which certain subjects are higher up in the hierarchy than others. The traditional subjects in our industrial schools have greater status –

such as science, maths, and languages. These 'prestigious' subjects are prioritised as they are seen to a highly desired, academic education that provide the primary route to a professional career and university. In the middle are the humanities and some subjects like the arts remain the 'Cinderellas' of all subjects where in some schools they are not addressed at all.

Also, firmly located on the bottom rung is a curious mixture of topics loosely called Personal, Social and Health education. I have always wondered how any meaningful education could be anything other than personal. This PSHE, although paid great lip service and scrutinised by the inspectorate, is organised in the UK on a pot-luck basis, often organised by a press gang, taught by the unwilling and received by the unenthusiastic. In reality, not much has changed since the initial curriculum of catastrophe that I delivered in the 70's, unless an individual school leader takes a lively and direct interest in this curricular area. Often it is poorly thought out, ineffectively delivered and coldly received. This is where the effective teaching of a carefully thought out well-being syllabus, delivered by an informed and interesting teacher, could be most effective.

Teachers are not amateur therapists. That was not their training and probably not their calling. It is time to return to an older viewpoint that we are teachers of pupils and not subjects. Any teacher worth her salt is interested in the all-round well-being of the pupils in her care. The best teachers are optimistic individuals who maximise the many chance opportunities that occur in each working day at school by noticing the chances to encourage their pupils and by acting on them. They recognise the special talents of their pupils, even if their enthusiasms and creative passions differ from the norm. They act as cheerleaders, encouraging their pupils for their effort and clever problem-solving strategies. They never offer empty praise to children because it is so detrimental and counter-productive to well-being. The best teachers are great facilitators of their pupils' learning and know what steps have to be taken next to ensure improvement. They see each child as an individual and set targets that stretch. They take on board Nelson Mandela's dictum 'It never hurts to think too highly of a person; often they become ennobled and act better because of it ...'

The reconstruction of what happens in schools can only improve with the revival of teachers who work there. Through the positive psychological principles offered here, most teachers can get more satisfaction from their work than they are gaining at the moment. A initial step forward would be to take action by reviewing their own signature strengths. By reviewing their own signature strengths they can organise their daily work in ways that promote a sense of optimal experience or flow state. By finding more gratification at work this will also reignite the flames of a dampened vocational calling.

In this book I argue that pupil well-being can be both a purpose and a function in contemporary school settings. Teaching becomes purposeful when specific, directed goals are established (*education for happiness*). This will take a concerted effort on behalf of those charged with the leadership of our schools. Orderliness is a pre-requisite for success. My first teaching experience described at the preface of this book confirms this.

The challenge for teachers is not to allow the well-being of their pupils and their raison d'etre, to become so implicit or hidden (e.g. an unplanned function) at a time when the main pressure point is on assessment or positioning on league tables. This latter aim should never have become a central purpose in the first place. Teachers teach to the test because their reputations are often staked on reports. We remember our best teachers because of their humanity and their acts of kindness. The impression of a good teacher with their genuine spark of charity, good humour always wins out in our consciousness over the government holy grail of better league table positioning. This truth will require a new sense of conviction and a new style of courage on the part of school leaders who will need to decide on priorities and then to decide what is it really worth fighting for.

Resilience in an Age of Austerity

There is a big difference between describing what is and suggesting what ought to be, and this is where this book takes the next step to demonstrate that :

1. There is general agreement that helping pupils to learn about well-being is the task of schools as well as families.

2. An emphasis on pupil well-being can enhance academic learning with pupils becoming calmer and more receptive

3. The benefits of well-being are measurable

4. A proven curriculum for well-being has been developed and is worthy of consideration

5. Pupils can be provided with a new set of skills, through a carefully planned well-being curriculum, that will have long term benefits that are scientifically demonstrable.

This book highlights the central part that teachers play in the social development of the pupils that attend their schools. McLaughlin and Clarke (2010) effectively remind us of the importance of the teacher pupil relationship over and beyond specific curricular provision.

> *'Our review of the literature suggests that the centrality of teacher-pupil relationships in the everyday experience of schooling is being underdeveloped and the lack of research on the development of practice is noteworthy. It is may be because it is seemingly more powerful to devise a programme of activities but the everyday and pervasive power of relationships to affect learning, social development and mental health would suggest this is not the best way forward. There is a need to develop the responsibility for the role that schools play in the psychosocial development of young people. Reforming the curriculum is not going to be sufficient. Relationships matter a great deal.'*

It can be argued that the case study school is so successful because of the commitment of its leadership to the teaching of well-being and because of the outstanding example of its lead teacher. The pupils in this study comment repeatedly about the expertise of their well-being teacher. This implies that the well-being of teachers is also highly significant and that the delivery of successful lessons in well-being can only occur if organizations are emotionally and psychologically intelligent.

This book has pointed the way to all kinds of straightforward and actionable findings. Money does little to make us happier after basic needs are met. If happiness is a mental state of being, then pupils should be able to control it through cognitive means. Temperamental set points account for a certain amount of our happiness but this is not an overwhelming percentage. Lyubormirsky (2008) suggests 40% of our happiness is within our control, whilst 10% is related to circumstances and 50% relates to our predisposition to stay at a certain level of happiness.

School is all about making our pupils better people. The good news is that change is an option. This is possible because we are not fatally pre-determined genetically or totally reliant on our environment for growth and personal development. The wisdom of Victor Frankl demonstrates that even in the worst circumstances there can be hope and a future. I am proposing a new logotherapy for 21st century schools where pupils can find new meaning in the pursuit of happiness. If all this sounds like awfully hard work, we should re-frame the focus on pupil well-being as the practice of strengths that will result in gratifications or flow: the intrinsic rewards can be substantial. On the part of teachers, a new vision is possible where our work engages us fully, draws on our strengths and immerses us in a sense of flow. For pupils, they learn to challenge their negative thoughts to improve a sense of well-being that comes from a new found resilience. These are just a few of the benefits as an alternative to the false allure of materialism. We cannot underestimate the hold that a materialistic lifestyle seems to have taken over our rationality in the important work of bringing up our children. In Oliver Sachs' words, 'Affluenza' is spreading. The 2011 UNICEF report seems to suggest that parents buy status, branded goods for their children as a protection against bullying whilst at the same time, their offspring's emotional needs are not being met. Parents feel compelled to buy their children these things, often against their better judgement. In this way we are perpetuating a joyless, consumer generation.

Between the pessimistic view that nothing can change us and the view that we can find a formula or an overriding monistic principle for positive change is a huge and messy space: it is here that the educational journeys of individuals are situated (Suissa 2009)

This book began with a reference to the UNICEF report on child well-being in rich countries, published in 2007, that spelled out in no uncertain terms, the depths that we are plumbing in this country in providing the basic psychological safety for our children. In its conclusion, the UNICEF report on child well-being (2011) was unanimous in its message: the path to well-being centres on time spent in families that are consistent and secure, enjoying good friendships, giving our children plenty of wholesome and educational activities to do, preferably resulting in time spent outdoors.

Give our children plenty of wholesome and educational activities to do, preferably outdoors.

In our busy world we are all called to assess how we live our lives. We have a tendency to live on automatic, to rush activities, to be solely focused on goals, to listen with only one ear: to exist in an unsatisfying sense of pre-occupation. Our amygdala response (a tendency towards 'fight or flight') always seems to be on high alert. We seem to have lost the means to switch off. We have increasingly lost a sense of well-being with an over-writing of experience by language based thoughts and plans. We have reduced those experiences that nourish us most physically and socially – enjoying a leisurely family meal together, for example.

We are struggling to give the children what they need. Boundaries and expectations that govern family life are not clearly defined in the UK. Participation in active and creative pursuits decrease by the time children reach secondary school.

It is difficult to see where the successful role models are coming from, given that we often learn best from example. Talking straight, it appears that in Britain today pornography has become the new sex education for the young, merely because of its accessibility through the internet. If liberal families are content to allow their children to be educated by popularist, gross-out entertainment in lieu of more time-costly family contact, then we cannot but expect that traditional values on which our civil society is based – respect, courtesy, manners, empathy, honesty, integrity – be lost. I would argue that such traditional values are the glue that gives us social cohesion or national identity.

We live in an argument culture where popular media depicts real life as a series of heated disagreements between individuals. Simply put, we appear to have lost a sense of the ability to reason with people we disagree with. Actions speak louder than words and if we disagree with social norms then who is there to stop us if we are forceful enough? The limits to the law were demonstrated vividly in London last Summer. There is a sense of entitlement in society that was seen in the mass civil disobedience in August 2011.

We have to face the sad and alarming truth that our children have a better relationship with their phone than their family. In so many ways Apple Corp. have captured the zeitgeist, the spirit of the 'i' world, where anything consensual goes and anyone who has the audacity to question anyone else's moral choices experiences wrath and anger.

Are we asking schools to do too much to deliver an effective programme for pupil well-being? Is pupil well-being easier to deliver to primary school children? Is this purely an urban model for education? These are all important issues for further research. What is clear is that the well-being of pupils constitutes a long term project that is vital to improving attainment. The expectations of pupils as well as families and employers have to be addressed. This requires a new way of looking at how school leaders and teachers work as they attempt to follow their best instincts.

In the interim we need to find a greater sense of interdependence. Although our young people give us a false sense of being masters of their own destiny in their command and control centres, based on the modern technologies found in their bedrooms, they are more connected at one level yet really know very few, and are thus truly alone.

To be a good parent demands a high level of creativity. In our pursuit of happiness we need to encourage our youngsters to connect with people around them, thinking of these connections as the cornerstones of their life (see neweconomics.org). Building these connections will support and enrich them. Prof. Felicia Huppert and her colleagues, in their book 'Flourishing across Europe' have produced convincing evidence to show that other key elements for contemporary well-being include discovering a physical activity that people enjoy and that suits their level of mobility and fitness. We all need to take notice more, be curious, savour the moment, to catch sight of the beautiful and to remark on the unusual. Keeping a simple gratitude diary will encourage us to reflect and appreciate the things that matter most.

Above all else we need to keep learning and try something new. When was the last time we tried something for the first time? Setting a challenge that we will enjoy achieving will keep our approach to life fresh, vital and authentic. Encountering new experiences will also help us grow in confidence as we face different conditions in austerity Britain.

What we want, above all else, is for our children to flourish, to be their best selves. Recently, Governments have begun to show that they have got the message that a sense of subjective well-being counts, by realising that a growth in Gross Domestic Product does not warrant a growth in personal well-being, and that new measures have to be envisaged. The promotion of a sustainable sense of well-being is well within our grasp, where we encourage our children to feel good, to function effectively as well as deal with negative emotions (that inevitably arise in life) by dealing with them effectively. This is the fruit of a resilient approach to life.

It is time to concentrate our energies on promoting the key elements of well-being in schools and homes – positive engagement; meaning; optimism; positive relationships; competence; vitality; resilience; emotional stability. In schools, we need to recognise that positive mental states broaden and build cognitive processes, that pupils in a positive mood have a broader focus of attention, are more creative, more resilient, are generous with time and resources and are more tolerant of others. Surely this is the glue that will create a more cohesive and creative Britain as we seek a way forward from austerity to well-being?

The best news of all is that our quality of life is not inextricably bound to the popular mythology about what constitutes an acceptable standard of living. It is possible that the current fall in living standards should not, of necessity, make us unhappier people. We might become wiser, in that recession provides a new and previously unexplored opportunity to rediscover the old truths about the emptiness of a purely materialistic life, along with the possibilities of actively encountering a new spiritual dimension to our understanding. According to the science of Positive Psychology, it is this quest for meaning that will bring greatest life satisfaction and well-being, not the next episode of retail therapy for the rich or the theft of a wide-screen by a hoodie.

Furthermore, there is no inevitability about a recession of values or virtues despite living in reduced circumstances. As teachers and members of the wider community, we have a new goal to direct our public service, namely to ensure that as many people as possible flourish, develop their full creative potential and are mindful of themselves as well as the needs of others. Talking straight, the alternative strategy is bleak as we witness the current reductionist schema of many of the politicians, aimed solely at surviving the current economic downturn. Some might say that we all seem to be waiting for the ship to right itself, impotent and powerless to take any active steps to improve conditions. This seems both to be an unworthy occupation and pre-occupation.

To realise our vision in schools means seeing beyond the blinkered limitations of taking seriously only those things that can be measured by league tables, focussed on exam results. It means spending time creatively in the preparation and delivery of a meaningful curriculum that is taught by a passionate and lively team of teachers, who recognise in turn the wider value of the work that they are engaged in with the young. If this vision of compassion is realised then we will have played a part in creating a new agenda of thriving in society and our idealistic dreams that we had in the late seventies, presented in the opening lines of this book, will be finally realised.

A Selected Bibliography:

Barclay, J. and Doll, B. (2001) Early prospective studies of high school dropout, School Psychology Quarterly, 16, 357- 69

Bassey, M. (1999) Case Study Research in Educational Settings. Buckingham: Open University.

Bentham, J. (1970) An introduction to the principles of morals and legislation Darien CT: Hafner (original work published 1789)

Blum, R. and Libbey, H. (2004) School connectedness- strengthening health and education outcomes for teenagers. Journal of School Health, 74, 231-2

Bond, L., Patton, G., Glover, S., Carlin, J.B., Butler, H., Lyndal Thomas, L. and Bowes, G. (2004) The Gatehouse Project: can a multilevel school intervention affect emotional well-being and health risk behaviours? Journal of Epidemiology and Community Health, 58, 997-1003

Bowen, N. and Bowen, G. (1998) The effects of home micro system risk factors and school micro system protective factors ion student academic performance and affective investment in schooling. Social Work in Education, 20, 219-231

Bowlby, J. (1969) Attachment and Loss. Volume 1. London Hogarth Press

Bryman, A. (2001) Social Research Methods. Oxford: Oxford University Press.

Callaway, R. (1979) Teachers' Beliefs Concerning Values and the Functions and Purposes of Schooling, Eric Document Reproduction Service No. ED 177 110

Catalano, R., Kostelman, R., Hawkins, J. (1996) Modeling the Etiology of Adolescent Substance Use: A Test of the Social Development Model, Journal of Drug Issues, 26(2): 429–455.

Claxton, G. (2008). What's the point of school? Re-discovering the Heart of Education. Oxford: OneWorld.

Collishaw S, Maughan B, Goodman R and Pickles A (2004) Time trends in adolescent mental health. Journal of Child Psychology and Psychiatry, Vol 45,

Csikszentmihalyi, M (1999) *If we are so rich, why are'nt we happy?* American Psychologist.

Diener, E. & Lucas, R. E. 2000 Subjective emotional well-being. In Handbook of emotions (ed. M. Lewis & J. M. Haviland-Jones), pp. 325–337. New York: Guilford.

Doll, B. and Hess, R. (2001) Through a new lens: contemporary psychological perspectives onschool completion and dropping out of high school. School Psychology Quarterly, 16, 351-6

DCSF Children's Plan (2007)

Durlak, JA. and Wells, A.M. (1997) Primary Prevention Mental Health Programs for Children and Adolescents: A Meta-Analytic Review, American Journal of CommunityPsychology, 25, (2), 115-152

Ehrenreich, B (2009) 'Bright-Sided: How the Relentless Promotion of Positive Thinking Has Undermined America' New York: Metropolitan Books

Emmons RA, McCullough M E (2003) *Counting Blessings Versus Burdens: An Experimental Investigation of Gratitude and Subjective Well-Being in Daily Life* Journal of Personality and Social Psychology, American Psychological Association, , Vol. 84, No. 2, 377–389

Eccles, J., Early, D., Frasier, K. and Belansky, E. (1997) The Relation of Connection, Regulation, and Support for Autonomy to Adolescents' Functioning. Journal of Adolescent Research, 12, 263-286

Ennals, Sir P (2009) Well-being, Schools and the system, lecture given at the British Museum, 24.10.09, NCB National Conference.

Finn, JD. (1993) School Engagement & Students at Risk, Washington; National Center for Education Statistics

Finn, JD. (1997) Academic success among students at risk for school failure. *Journal of Applied Psychology* 82(2): 221-34

Gilbert, Daniel (2006), *Stumbling on Happiness*, Knopf

Glover, S., Burns, J., Butler, H. and Patton, G. (1998) Social environments and the emotional well-being of young people. Family Matters, 49, 11-16

Hammond, Sue Annis (1998) 2nd edition The Thin Book of Appreciative Inquiry, Thin Book Publishing Company

Healthy Weight, Healthy Lives: A Cross-Government Strategy for England (2008) published by the Department for Health

Huppert, A.F. et al (2009). Measuring well-being across Europe: Description of the ESS Well-being Module and preliminary findings. Social Indicators Research, 91, 301-315.

Kessler, R. C., McGonagle, K. A., Zhao, S., Nelson, C. B., Hughes, M., Eshelman, S., Wittchen, H. & Kendler, K. S. 1994 Lifetime and 12-month prevalence of DSM-III-R psychiatric disorders in the United States. Arch. Gen. Psychiatry 51, 8–19.

Lee, T.D. (1992) Health of the Nation? Enquiry into the increase of smokers in teen-aged females Unpublished paper, Cambridge University School of Education, M.Ed,

Leeson, P (2009) Pupils' well-being in the 21st Century school The role of Ofsted in promoting improvement in schools, lecture given at the British Museum, 14 October 2009.

Libbey, H. (2004) Measuring Student Relationships to School: Attachment, Bonding, Connectedness, and Engagement. Journal of School Health, 74, 274-82

Lyubomirsky, S. (2008). *The how of happiness: A scientific approach to getting the life you want*. New York: Penguin Press.

Marcus, R. and Sanders-Reio, J. (2001) The influence of attachment on school completion. School Psychology Quarterly, 16, 427-44.

Marks, H. (2000) Student Engagement in Instructional Activity: Patterns in the Elementary,Middle, and High School Years. American Educational Research Journal, Spring 2000, 37 (1), 153-184

Mayall, B. (2007) Children's Lives Outside School and their Educational Impact. The Cambridge Primary Review Briefing Report 8/1.

McLaughlin, C and Clarke, B Relational Matters: a review of the impact of school experience on mental health in early adolescence Educational and Child Psychology, 27, (1). (in print, 2010)

McNeely, CA., Nonnemaker, JM. and Blum, RW. (2002) Promoting School Connectedness: Evidence from the National Longitudinal Study of Adolescent Health. Journal of School Health, 72, (4) 138-146.

Morris, I (2009) Learning to elephants: Teaching Happiness and Well-being in Schools Continuum: London

Newmann, F. (1992) Student Engagement and Achievement in American Secondary Schools. New York: Teachers College Press.

Nuffield Foundation (2004) Time trends in adolescent well-being

Patton, M.Q. (2002) Qualitative research and Evaluation Methods. Thousand Oaks, CA: Sage.

Pennebaker, J. W. (1997). Opening up: The healing power of expressing emotions. New York: Guilford Press

Pert, C. (199) *Molecules Of Emotion: The Science Between Mind-Body Medicine* New York: Scribner

Peters, T Waterman R, (1986) In search of excellence Warner: New York

Peterson, C.,Park, N. & Seligman,M.E.P. 2005 Approaches to happiness: the full life versus the empty life. Unpublished manuscript, University ofMichigan. Am. Psychol. (Submitted.)

Pople, L. (2009) The Good Childhood Inquiry: What Children Told Us, London: Children's Society.

Punch, K. (1998) Introduction to Social Research. London: Sage.

Reddy, R., Rhodes, J. and Mulhall, P. (2003) 'The influence of teacher support on student adjustment in the middle school years: a latent growth curve study', Development and Psychopathology, 15, 119-138.

Resnick, MD., Harris, LJ. and Blum, RW. (1993) The impact of caring and connectedness on adolescent health and well-being. Journal of Paediatrics and Child Health, 29(1), 3-9.

Resnick, MD., Bearman, PS., Blum, RW. and Bauman, KE. (1997) Protecting adolescents from harm. Findings from the National Longitudinal Study on Adolescent Health. Journal of the American Medical Association, 278, 823-32

Resnick, MD. (2000) Protective factors, resiliency and healthy youth development. Adolescent Medicine, 11(1), 157-65

Resnick M. (2005) Healthy youth development: Getting our priorities right. Medical Journal of Australia, 183(8):398-400

Robinson, K. and Aronica, L. (2009) The Element How finding your passion changes everything. Penguin: London

Roeser, RW., Eccles, JS. and Sameroff, AJ. (2000) School as a context of early adolescents' academic and social-emotional development; a summary of the research findings. The Elementary School Journal. 100,5, 443-471

Roeser, R.W., Eccles, J.S. & Strobel, K. (1998). Linking the study of schooling and mental health: Selected issues and empirical illustrations at the level of the individual. Educational Psychologist, 33, 153-176.

Rosenfeld, LB., Richman, JM. and Bowen, GL. (2000) Social Support Networks and School Outcomes: The Centrality of the Teacher. Child and Adolescent Social Work Journal, 17, (3), 204-226

Roberts, Y (2009). *Grit: The Skills for Success and How They Are Grown.* London: The Young Foundation.

Rudduck, J. and Flutter, J. (2004) Consulting pupils: what's in it for schools? London: Routledge.

Rutter, M. (1991) 'Pathways to and from childhood to adult life: the role of schooling.' Pastoral Care in Education, 9 (3), 3-10

Rutter, M. and Smith, D. (1995) Psychosocial Disorders in Young People: Time Trends and Their Causes, Chichester: John Wiley.

Suissa, J. (2009). Lessons from a new science? On teaching happiness in schools. In Cigman R and Davis A (Eds.) *New Philosophies of Learning* pp 205 – 220. Chichester: John Wiley & Sons.

Seligman, M. (1993) What you can change and what you can't. New York: Knopf.

Seligman, M. (2002) Authentic happiness. New York: Free Press.

Seligman, M ((2011) *Flourish A new Understanding of Happiness and Well-being and how to achieve them*. London: Nicholas Brearley

Seligman, M. E. P. & Steen, T. 2005 Making people happier: a randomized controlled study of exercises that build positive emotion, engagement, and meaning. Am. Psychol. (Submitted.)

Smith D.J and Rutter M. (1995) Time trends in psychosocial disorders of youth. In M Rutter and DJ Smith (eds) Psychosocial disorders in young people: Time trends and their causes. Chichester: Wiley

Smith, D. (2006) 'School Experience and Delinquency at Ages 13 to 16,' Edinburgh Study of Youth Transitions and Crime, number 13. Edinburgh Centre for Law and Society, University of Edinburgh, UK.

Stake, R. (1994) 'Case Studies'. In: Denzin, N. and Lincoln, Y. eds. (1994) Handbook of Qualitative Research. Thousand Oaks, CA: Sage.

Steinberg, L. (1996) Beyond the Classroom: Why school reform has failed and what parents need to do. New York: Simon and Schuster.

Vostanis, P. (2007) 'Mental health and mental disorders,' in J. Coleman and A. Hagell (2007)Adolescence Risk and resilience: against the odds. Chichester: John Wiley and Sons Ltd.

Weare, K. and Gray, G. (2003) What Works in Developing Children's Emotional and Social Well-being? Research Report RR456. London: Department for Education and Skills

Wentzel. K. R. (1998) School Relationships and Motivation in Middle School: The Role of Parents, Teachers and Peers *Journal of Educational Psychology*, 90, (2), pp. 202-209